What
to Do
When *the*

ECONOMY
SUCKS

What
When to Do
the

ECONOMY
SUCKS

101

Tips to Help You Hold On
to **Your Job**, **Your House**,
and **Your Lifestyle!**

PETER SANDER

332.024
965

A BUSINESS
Avon, Massachusetts

Published by Adams Business, an imprint of
Adams Media, a division of F+W Media, Inc.
57 Littlefield Street, Avon, MA 02322. U.S.A.
www.adamsmedia.com

ISBN-10: 1-60550-095-X
ISBN-13: 978-1-60550-095-9

Printed in Canada.

J I H G F E D C B A

Library of Congress Cataloging-in-Publication Data
is available from the publisher.

This publication is designed to provide accurate and authoritative information
with regard to the subject matter covered. It is sold with the understanding
that the publisher is not engaged in rendering legal, accounting, or other professional advice. If legal advice or other expert assistance is required, the services of a competent professional person should be sought.
 —From a *Declaration of Principles* jointly adopted by a Committee of the
American Bar Association and a Committee of Publishers and Associations

Many of the designations used by manufacturers and sellers to distinguish
their product are claimed as trademarks. Where those designations appear in
this book and Adams Media was aware of a trademark claim, the designations
have been printed with initial capital letters.

This book is available at quantity discounts for bulk purchases.
For information, please call 1-800-289-0963.

Dedication

I dedicate *What to Do When the Economy Sucks* to all hardworking individuals and families who have the serenity to accept financial conditions they cannot change, the will to change the things they can, and the wisdom to know the difference. Not surprisingly, this book is designed to help you change the things you can and deal with the rest as best possible.

Acknowledgments

A lot of folks deserve credit as role models, but I'd especially like to recognize my parents Jerry and Betty Sander, now deceased, who taught me frugal living at an early age, how to play financial defense (and why!), and how not to sweat the financial small stuff. I should also thank my family, namely Jennifer and boys Julian and Jonathan, for their prudence with money and tolerance for my spending yet another summer writing a book.

Contents

Introduction...1

Part I: Hold On to Your Job...9

Chapter 1. The Art of Hanging On...11

How to play defense in your job, how to become more valuable to your organization in your existing role, how to achieve just a little more and market it more effectively in your organization to immunize yourself from upcoming layoffs.

Chapter 2. Improving the Merchandise...27

Hanging on to your job is one thing, finding another within your industry or outside your industry is another matter. How to make yourself more valuable to the broader job market, acquiring new skills, learning new businesses or industries, making yourself visible, using the network, working with recruiters.

Chapter 3. The Other Side of the Fence...43

Yes, the grass may be greener. Maybe it's time for a bigger change—time to work for yourself? This option can make a lot of sense in a downturn, if handled right. How to decide if the entrepreneurship/solopreneurship option is right for you, and how to prepare for it.

Chapter 4. If the Ax Falls...57

How to cope with the change and the transition, what to do next, how to keep your financial and emotional wits about you, what to do, and what not to do.

Part II: Hold On to Your Home...69

Chapter 5. Time for a Crash Diet?...71

Losing a home can be one of the hardest things to deal with both financially and emotionally. This chapter gives tips for pulling out all the stops to keep making those mortgage or rent payments on time.

Chapter 6. Renegotiate, Refinance, but Don't Renege...85

A look at the anatomy and timing of the foreclosure process, who the parties are in the process, and how you can work a deal with them if the cards line up right. Government programs to help those in mortgage trouble are also described.

Chapter 7. Moving On When You Must...103

Sometimes it just doesn't make financial or emotional sense to keep beating your head against a housing-related wall. Tips on how to sell your home and make a sensible relocation decision, how to make the best of a bad situation.

Part III: Hold On to Your Lifestyle...121

Chapter 8. Financial Forensics...123

Where does the money go? This chapter explains how to take a hard, objective, and actionable look at what you spend money on and why. The idea being, of course, to learn how, as a family unit, to cut the waste and spend smart.

Chapter 9. Should You Live on a Budget?...139

Everyone hates to budget, but it doesn't have to be so bad. The word "budget" is usually equated with "detail" and "control," neither of which are very appetizing ideas in family finance. This chapter shows how to make big-picture budgeting work to preserve your lifestyle, and improve it in better economic times.

Chapter 10. Smart Debt, Smart Credit...153

In a downturn, how you manage debt and use credit will influence your lifestyle more than ever. How to do the right things, avoid common debt problems, improve credit, and recover from a debt crisis.

Chapter 11. Protect Your Ass(ets)...171

A bad economy can not only knock a hole in your income, but also your wealth base—your investments. How to protect your savings and investments, including retirement investments, and how to make the most of your investments in a down economy.

Chapter 12. Downsize with Dignity...189

Small defenses might help, but sometimes a bigger solution or readjustment is in order. How to migrate to a less costly lifestyle that is just as fulfilling—or even more fulfilling—than before.

Introduction

The headlines won't go away. Anywhere, everywhere, in the paper, on the web, on television news. All grim.

"Initial jobless claims were 373,000 last week, far more than economists had expected, and the unemployment rate edged up to the highest level in three years."

"Durable goods orders fell 2.5 percent, and factory orders resumed their year-long slump."

"Consumer confidence fell to the lowest level in almost 5 years."

"The stock market dropped 777 points on fresh worries about the financial sector."

"Consumer prices shot up by a record 1.5 percent last month, while housing starts fell to a new 3-year low."

"Consumer debt rose last month to the highest level ever."

"Foreclosures were up a stunning 33 percent from the same time last year, and show no signs of abating."

Somebody make it stop, please.

If It Walks, Talks, and Acts Like a Duck . . .

When you hear this sort of news, you know the economy sucks. And now it comes closer to home. Your next-door neighbor's car is in the driveway at 9:30 on Tuesday morning. You finally get up the nerve to ask. A pink slip last Friday. Your young child's best friend no longer shows up at the Montessori school—because the parents can't afford it. Your other neighbor just sold his boat at a

1

fire-sale price—needs the money to get his furnace fixed and pay this winter's heating bills.

You feel your business—your company—slowing down. Less overtime, fewer rosy revenue projections. Nobody's talking about expanding the building or adding a new location. Everyone's talking about downsizing. If you're in a public agency, your funding is being cut. Things aren't growing anymore or even staying the same. Everything feels slower and smaller.

Your job is probably at risk. Less income, no income—yikes! Of course, your bills won't get laid off; they'll keep coming. They may even get bigger. Finding a new job costs money, too.

And depending on what is making the economy suck, everyday items like gas and food and visits to the doctor or dentist are getting more expensive. Less income, no income, higher costs.

You feel vulnerable, now more than ever. Even if the "real" economy—the world economy, the U.S. economy, the local economy—isn't so bad, your personal economy can suck. It can be the economy in your line of work, as so many found out years ago in the steel industry, or more recently, in the auto industry, or still more recently, in the newspaper, real estate, and construction industries.

Or something on the "cost" side, like an unexpected medical bill, can make your own personal economy "suck," even if everyone else's seems okay.

The point is—it really doesn't matter what the economists and talking heads call it. It might be a "recession" or a "downturn." Whatever; the experts never agree anyway. Technically, a "recession" is defined as "two or more calendar quarters of negative GDP" growth. But as we all found out in the 2007–2008 downturn, the economy can suck long before those two quarters of negative growth are rung up.

Whether or not the economy officially sucks doesn't really matter, anyway. If *your* economy sucks, it's time for action. That action is what this book is about.

What Is Defensive Personal Finance?

This is a personal finance book. "Finance" because it's about money, "personal" because it's about *your* money. What are most personal finance books about? Look at the titles: how to become a millionaire, how to get rich, how to have a great retirement. They're about making money, increasing wealth, or saving money for something.

This book is different; it's not about making money at all. I'm going to tackle a different issue: keeping what you have, preserving your lifestyle, preserving the home you've worked so hard for, and preserving your job in order to preserve those other things. I call it defensive personal finance.

Defensive personal finance is about the financial actions and attitudes necessary for you and your family to preserve your job (and thus your income), your home, and most of all, your lifestyle. Defensive personal finance is based on the assumption that you've gotten where you are through hard work. You've managed to build a career, acquire a home (whether through renting or buying), and achieve a lifestyle you're comfortable with. Sure, you may have longer-term financial goals like a boat or larger home that you're still pursuing, but those things may or may not happen right away.

But you don't want to take a step backward because of a sucky economy. The point right now is to play defense, to keep bad things from sucking away the support for the lifestyle you're already living. That includes the retirement lifestyle you've already earned and plan to live. Economic turmoil may push that boat or that second home further into the future, but that's not what this book is about—it's about preserving what you have, what you've achieved, with minimum stress and anxiety.

That last sentence is important. Financial stress and strife are the number one cause of marital and family stress and strife. The ramifications of a sucky economy can go far beyond bank accounts—they can change lives in a big way.

The 101 actionable tips I give will help you circle the wagons to preserve what you have, financially and emotionally. That's the number one objective, and I hope you come away feeling a little stronger and less vulnerable to the world's troubles.

If followed, much of the advice in this book will also help you build wealth when times are better. Good personal finance means always looking ahead. If the economy, or your economy, doesn't suck right at the moment, it always helps to look ahead. Playing defense means anticipating what might happen so you can be prepared to deal with it. The business types would call it being proactive.

A Little Perspective on Downturns

Although it may seem that way every time one happens, economic downturns are hardly a new thing.

Human nature turns us all (most of us, anyway) into optimists—especially when things are good. We make more, have more, and, hopefully, save more. Our decisions are reinforced by success, whether it's from buying a home, investing in the stock market, or taking a new job. Things work out for the best, and we feel good about ourselves, our ability to make financial decisions, our influence on financial outcomes.

Then the economy tanks.

Naturally, a Cycle

Downturns are a normal part of what's known as the "economic cycle." The economy has, in fact, logged nine recessions from 1950 through 2001. The economists don't agree (yet) on 2007–2008, but I'll make the call—it counts as Number Ten. That's about one recession every six years.

True, the frequency has dropped somewhat. Better government policy at the Federal Reserve level, plus radically improved business and personal productivity brought on by technology, gave unusually long periods of prosperity from March 1991 through March 2001, and again from late 2002 into 2008. If you're under forty, you probably only remember the "dot-bomb" drop of 2001–2002; the previous downturn around Gulf War I happened when you were in college or just starting work life. Other than that, you only hear about downturns from your parents and grandparents.

The point is, recessions happen, and the cycle is pretty consistent. Something happens to shake business confidence, consumer confidence, or both. In 2001 it was the collapse of the overvalued dot.com stocks, followed by the September 11, 2001, terrorist attacks. In 2007–2008 it was the contraction in the real-estate market and tightening credit.

Some commodity shock, some credit shock or bankruptcy, some political problem, or some combination of these and other factors is usually responsible. It's more likely to happen just after things are good, as good times have a tendency to magnify bad times when the herd all turn in another direction at once. Downturns do happen and always will happen.

Shorter Than You Think

Just like your personal life, when things are bad, they seem to take longer—forever, in fact. That 2001–2002 dot.com recession seemed like it would never end. Some structural changes, brought on by increased productivity and—worse—a lot of offshoring of key jobs, caused some of its effects to linger to this day—which is why many call it a jobless recovery.

Yes, downturns do tend to have lingering effects. But some of them are good—the 1973–1975 oil-shock downturn brought greater fuel efficiency and awareness of energy problems. The Great Depression brought greater bank regulation and overall government protection against financial things gone wrong. The 2007–2008 downturn contributed more rational lending standards and realistic real estate prices.

And for the most part, the pain is short lived. As measured by the stock market, only one of the nine recessions since 1950 lasted longer than a year—the one in 1973–1975. Government intervention and good old hard work usually serve to get us out of a recession. According to the Bureau of Labor Statistics, the average duration of unemployment in June 2008 is 17.5 weeks; only one-third of unemployed are unemployed for longer than four months; only one-fifth for longer than six months.

Most recessions have a silver lining, for example, the export boom during the 2007–2008 downturn. So as bad as things may seem, we can take solace in the fact that recessions usually last less than a year, and are accompanied by much longer boom periods.

"What DO You Do When the Economy Sucks?"

Simple, straightforward question, and I heard it over and over as I contacted friends and colleagues in developing this book, Always their first question. So before we start, here's the short answer:

- ✔ *Don't ignore.* When things go bad with money, relationships, health, or life in general we have a tendency to look the other way, to consider it a mere speed bump. "It'll go away," right? But ignoring job security or debt obligations or misplaced retirement assets is like closing your eyes while driving in a night rainstorm—it just makes the problem worse.
- ✔ *Don't panic.* On the other hand, knee-jerk reactions will almost guarantee the wrong outcomes. You'll sell a house or investments at ridiculous lows. You'll lose gains or savings you've fought for for years. The emotional turbulence causes collateral damage in family, work, and much of the rest of your life. Keep a level head, evaluate the facts and alternatives.
- ✔ *Get the family involved.* Going it alone doesn't work. Your family is part of the team and part of the solution. Get everyone on board in making decisions and putting them into play.
- ✔ *Take positive steps.* Build a "moat" around your job. Protect your home. Cut back spending, make the tough choices. Just do it. You'll feel more secure, you'll feel better. The 101 tips that follow give the whats, whys, and hows.

✔ *Learn the lessons.* Sucky economies mean adjustments for most families. You're not alone. Learn from them and adjust living standards for the long term if necessary. Make sure your kids learn too so they can handle bad stuff years down the road.

Three Defensive Fronts: Your Job, Your Home, Your Lifestyle

What to Do When the Economy Sucks isn't intended as a dry, dull, cover-to-cover financial read, but rather one where you can "helicopter" into the issue that concerns you most and lift out some handy, practical financial advice.

Good luck!

Part I

Hold On to Your Job

Chapter 1

The Art of Hanging On

In the realm of defensive personal finance, nothing is more important than preserving your income. Unless you're lucky enough to be sitting on a pile of wealth or have specific plans to inherit some soon, income is what makes your financial world go 'round. Why? Because unless you're living at home with your parents under some kind of special (and likely difficult) arrangement, you have expenses. And when you have expenses, and no means to pay for them, debt is inevitable. You borrow from tomorrow to pay for today.

Of course, that doesn't work for the long term. The reasons are obvious—tomorrow you'll have to pay for today—and whatever expenses you incur tomorrow. When the economy sucks, preserving your income is the first front to defend in the war for your personal finances. Above all, that means maneuvering the troops into position to keep your job.

FROM THE CORPORATE POINT OF VIEW

What do corporations do when the economy sucks? A 2008 survey of 1,389 companies worldwide (275 in the U.S.) showed what companies do to cut back during tough times:

- 52 percent lay off employees
- 46 percent restructure their organization
- 39 percent grant smaller raises
- 13 percent freeze salaries
- 9 percent set up an early retirement window
- 8 percent reduce the workweek

Source: Watson Wyatt Worldwide, published in the *Wall Street Journal*

It's All about Value—Your Value

The first line of defense in defending your job is not only to preserve but to enhance your value to your employer. Sure, people get laid off in tough times; businesses (and public or nonprofit agencies, too) change even in a good economy. In a bad economy, when sales and revenues suck, a business shifts focus to control what it can—its costs. Regardless of how you perceive your value to the business, you are a cost.

Here's another truth: All of your coworkers and other employees of the enterprise are costs, too. When management turns its attention to the wheat and the chaff in your organization, the trick is to make sure you're the wheat. You want to make sure you are the best—and perceived as the best—soldier on the line. When push comes to shove, if life is at all rational (and sometimes it isn't), you'll be the soldier they keep.

Don't Be Good—Be Great

Here's a myth: "Good" employees will be kept on board. Don't spend too much time hiding behind that one. "Bad" employees can be fired or lost through attrition, and nobody asks questions; in fact, everyone agrees it's the right thing for the boss to do. And "great" employees? Self-explanatory.

The merely good employee? They can be a boss's worst nightmare. Some do good work once in a while, but waste time, could have done things better, could have presented it better. In good times, they might be tolerated. Maybe they'll get better, maybe the boss can get some value out of them, but they're a lot of work, they're "high maintenance." When times are tough, it's easier to make them go away. Being "good" won't be good enough.

The tips in this chapter will help tune up your work—that is, the quality and style of your work and the perception of that work—so you will be perceived as a "most valuable player" in your organization. That won't guarantee anything, but in times of trouble, it will help protect your job. Not only that, it's bound to lead to better things when the economy no longer sucks.

Tip #1: Be the MVP

Who is the Most Valuable Player in any given sports league? On the surface, she's the person who contributes the most to the team's success, its winning record, its recognition as the best team in the league. But an MVP also, by virtue of his or her skills, attitude, and leadership, makes the rest of the team better. We're not only talking about the other players, but the coaches and even the folks in the front office.

Why Is It Important?

There's nothing better than establishing yourself as an MVP in the workplace. You become the "go-to" guy for all that matters to the organization. As the go-to person in your organization, you're less likely to get the boot. And just as obviously, when times get better, you'll be first in line for the raise, the promotion, the recognition that will shine the light down your career path for years to come.

Of course, becoming an MVP is no simple task. It requires a well-blended combination of skills, attitude, accomplishment, leadership, and diplomacy.

What to Do

Make your boss look great. Michael Jordan and Scottie Pippen, and more recently Kobe Bryant, put up some pretty good NBA numbers and led their teams to glory. But they also did something else along the way—they made coach Phil Jackson look great; in fact, one of the winningest coaches in NBA history. Now, don't you think Mr. Jackson would do almost anything to keep these guys on his roster? You bet.

In your workplace, you should always think about what makes your boss look good. "Make your boss look like a genius," says executive recruiter Mark Jaffe, "and everything else will fall into place." What makes your boss look good makes your organization look good, too. And nothing can be better than having your boss—and her boss—protect you. And yet, how many times, especially in the nervous clutches of uncertainty, do we fume about the boss and doubt her skills? Get over it. Make your boss a genius. Anticipate the needs of the business. Do great stuff on time (or early) and flawlessly. Get those tough customer wins. Above all, be creative and positive.

Be a clutch performer. Do well—especially when the chips are down and it counts. And here's another tip: Do what no one else will do. Solve ugly problems. Take on sticky projects. Deal with the tough clients or customers. Most Valuable Players can take over a game, and they can usually do things that no one else can—or wants to—do. It's all part of being indispensable.

Make other team members look better. Most organizations have stars—individuals who know the job, the technology, and the processes better than everyone else. They're the go-to individuals when the server goes down or when the organization is confronted with a difficult problem. In time and with training, others in the organization can learn these roles. The true MVP strives to make others in the organization better, too. Kobe Bryant learned to pass, not just shoot, making his other team members better, and earned MVP status for the first time in 2008. So, helping your boss get the most out of your team will help you achieve MVP status.

Tip #2: Work Like a Well-Oiled Machine

As you know from your own life, when things are tense, even the little things really bug you. It's the same for your boss; so put yourself in his shoes. He'll be annoyed if he's holding a meeting and you walk in ten minutes late and still sweating from your lunchtime workout. And your boss is likely to be upset if he's trying to get the last touches of a proposal together and you're standing at the water cooler talking about your weekend plans. So don't be the slacker; be the reliable, helpful employee. If you're on time, organized, and exploding with productive energy, you've marked yourself as someone on the upward path.

Why Is It Important?

All else being equal, if it comes down to a choice between you and another employee, the boss is going to favor the employee who is the most efficient and productive— and the least irritating or annoying. If you're a time waster, your departure will bring relief to your boss. And if the boss needs a reason to let you go instead of your comparable coworker—well, there you go.

What to Do

Be punctual. You may have learned or heard about the 4 Ps—patience, perseverance, preparation, punctuality. This last one's important. Punctuality gives your boss—and the rest of the organization—the sense that you're organized and that you're about them, not yourself. If you've lapsed into the "All meetings start late" or "I'm sure they'll wait for me" mode, lapse out of it.

Be dependable. It goes with punctuality, but on a larger scale. When a boss can count on you, especially in crunch time, you're an asset. If not, you're a liability.

Be consistent. Consistent work quality, consistent attendance, and the ability to be there and ready at crunch time are highly valued. If they aren't there, you're more of a liability than an asset. Remember, bosses appreciate those who can boss themselves most.

Take care of distractions. "My kid forgot his lunch again." "The swimming pool contractor's coming at 3:00 P.M.; gotta be there." Cell phones and e-mail blasting forth with personal this and that, friends coming by to discuss yesterday's NFL game, etc. Bosses notice; they don't have time for this stuff, so why should you?

Tip #3: Master Reading, 'Riting, and Rhetoric

Most jobs require a set of basic (or advanced) technical skills to get the work done. You learn them through a combination of education, training, and experience. And every organization has its task superstars who can get the job done with all i's dotted and t's crossed. If you're the organization's taskmaster, you have a leg up. But if you can't communicate or keep up with the outside world, that could spell trouble.

Why Is It Important?

People not only notice good work—they notice those who can articulate, communicate, and sell that work inside and outside the organization. They recognize those who not only can do the work, but who know their work so well they become the go-to for everyone else. Sometimes they help accomplish a task, but just as often they help communicate, positioning or advocating the work to someone else. It's not just solutions—great employees can add value by articulating a *problem* to an organization.

So, you can build your value beyond the work itself by becoming an expert advocate, a spokesperson, a communicator for the organization.

What to Do

Be the informed one. Keep learning. Sure, you know your job well, but to get great at what you do and be recognized for it, keep current from an inside and outside perspective. Doctors, attorneys, accountants, and many others do continuing education to sharpen skills and stay fresh on the latest happenings "in the biz," so to speak. Do your own CE. Read trade pubs, watch online forums, take a course or two if related. Be the one to come in bright and fresh in the morning with, "Did you see that *Wall Street Journal* article on the latest new product in our industry?"

Sharpen your writing skills. Even if you do good work, if you write up the results like an eighth grader, you'll depreciate its value. Everyone should practice their writing so they can write material like it was to appear in a national newspaper or Internet column—in a short, crisp, correct style. Follow examples. Don't be shy—have a friend or even professional writer look at your stuff. Practice.

Speak now—or forever hold your peace. Bad speech, like bad writing, will subtract points from the value of good work. At best, it's distracting; at worst, no one will know what you're talking about, and your boss certainly won't send you on the road or into the public eye. Again, practice—and take a look at Toastmasters (*www.toastmasters.org*) for a chapter in your area. You'll build the skill in a nonthreatening environment.

BECOME A TALKING HEAD

One of my colleagues pestered me constantly about getting on TV to further my career. I was working for a big technology company at the time, and all of my speaking was to internal audiences—hardly TV material and hardly in TV mode. Fast forward to my writing career, and I was speaking on TV and radio a lot. Boy, did those experiences help me organize my thoughts and speak well under fire. Once I'd been through that, the average ten-minute conference-room pitch to a VP became a piece of cake. So, volunteer to be the spokesperson. Make a news interview appearance—or even a game show, if possible.

If nothing else, it gives you something cool to talk about at lunch.

Tip #4: Don't Stick Out

They work 8:00 A.M.–5:00 P.M. (or longer), take the standard forty-five minutes for lunch, sit in a modestly decorated cube, wear nice slacks, a dress shirt, and perhaps a jacket or tie or conservative monotone pants suit most of the time.

You, on the other hand, start work at 6:00 A.M., take a two-and-a-half-hour lunch to practice for your triathlon, then finish the day from 1:30 P.M. to 6:00 P.M.—and that's on one of your regular days. You sometimes telecommute, but on no kind of recognized schedule. You wear business casual every day, often a little more casual than business, and put on the tourist look on "casual Fridays." And your cube or office looks like a cross between a Haight-Ashbury drug den and a Victorian parlor, complete with bumper stickers touting your favorite political candidate.

Why Is It Important?

Okay, granted, the example is exaggerated. But the point is clear: With a few exceptions, regardless of your abilities and accomplishments, you don't want to stick out—especially in any way that can be perceived as negative. Why? Management's making hard choices, choices of who to downsize. In the absence of hard data about your performance (which is the case in many jobs), such silly things as what kind of shirts you wear can make the difference.

What to Do

Heed the culture. Work is about doing something for someone else in return for the compensation you covet. So you want to purvey the image that, yes, you're sacrificing your own interests to further theirs. That means meeting the rest of the organization and its culture on its turf, not yours. Fit in, be a good corporate citizen, be observant. Don't be the outlier, the office jester, the wag. You want the right kind of attention, not just attention.

Dress for success. Part of succeeding is dependent on how you look, not just what you do or how you behave. Some organizations have documented dress codes; if yours does, follow them. More subtle are the unwritten codes, which are usually obvious, but worth talking to a superior or two about if you have any lingering doubts. Sticking out like a sore thumb may not perpetuate long-term employment.

Spend company money like it's your own. On a business trip? Three cocktails before dinner, appetizers, a $29 rib-eye, dessert, and an after-dinner drink may be just reward for a successful day. Or is it? Likewise, renting the convertible or flying the most expensive flights just because you can will be noticed sooner or later. Employees who care for their employers are cared for in return, while greed and waste get their just rewards.

Tip #5: Stay Positive

Suppose you're a manager. You have two employees of equal caliber. One is the strong silent type, willing to be judged by actions and an occasional constructive comment. The other spends most of the day whining about this assignment, that employee, some aspect of her benefits package. At crunch time, who gets the boot?

Why Is It Important?

The ancient "power of positive thinking" mantra has a long history in the work environment. Like it or not, people feel good when others are positive, and uncomfortable and annoyed by those who aren't.

Sure, there are great employees who, because of native personality, stress, or intensity mix their great results with a lot of extracurricular angst, but they're the exception. Negative attitude spills over; others in the group, including bosses, start to become negative about negative people, and assume work quality or interactions with other employees and or customers is tainted by the bad attitude. It can become a vicious circle.

What to Do

Be easy to manage. Positive attitude, properly channeled energy, anticipation of what the boss wants, etc. Be the employee you would want to manage if you were your boss.

Don't whine about work or money. I had a coworker who bent my ear every chance he got about how the company misjudged his performance and was underpaying him. Another coworker caught the bug and spent hours telling me—repeatedly—how her benefits package wasn't up to snuff and how the company wouldn't offer benefits to part-time workers. She was about to launch an employee revolt over the topic. Whether she had a point or not, it was annoying to hear over and over about what the company should do for them. Remember, as John F. Kennedy would say, it's about what you can do for your company.

Listen, don't vent—especially about other people. Nobody likes to hear complaints about being underpaid, and nobody likes to hear constant blasts directed at coworkers. True or not, they're best kept to yourself. Why? It infects the group with negativity, and soon the boss assumes they're the subject of the abuse. There's really no good place for office gossip or employee bashing. Remember, smart bosses get rid of troublemakers first.

Be infectiously positive. Successful employees—and leaders—are not only positive, they imbue others with their positive attitudes. If you feel yourself making others around you more positive and energetic, that's a good thing. If you don't bring positive energy, you're vulnerable. Bosses notice.

Tip #6: Build Your Internal Brand

Brands, like Coca-Cola, Tide, and Starbucks, are important marketing tools. Not only are they recognizable, they also contain a brand promise—of quality, dependability, or service. Buyers know what they'll be getting and can depend on it; the brand becomes shorthand for soft drinks, detergent, and coffee shops. As an employee, you can build a brand, too. Not as another fictitious name like Tide or Coke, but for yourself, using your own name, as a dependable, go-to individual.

Why Is It Important?

Your manager and coworkers will begin to rely on you for your special expertise, and expertise leads to irreplaceability, which leads to job security. Just build a promise to your organization that you'll deliver consistent, reliable quality; innovative solutions; or customer management skills (to name a few examples). When your boss says, "I want Lewis for that job!" or "That project has the Lewis touch!" you're getting there.

What to Do

Be a model for consistency. Deliver consistent, high-quality work with your own distinctive style or trademark. That can be a visual or graphic style (as long as it's consistent with organizational norms) or a tendency toward brevity or getting the last but most observant word in a conversation.

Market your work—in writing, please. You can do the best work possible, but remember—those around you, including your boss, are busy people. They may not notice everything about it they should, so my favorite tactic is to write a short summary every two weeks or so for the boss and any interested coworkers. Include what you've done, what you're doing, and what challenges lie ahead. This can work even if you're a ditch digger—bosses like to keep up. It shows your dedication and puts a biweekly message with your brand.

Stay in touch—show up. In today's world of telecommuting, it's easy to get out of touch: out of sight, out of mind. You may be doing good work, but soon your coworkers start to suspect you're really doing yard work. So even if you work remotely, make a point of showing up once in a while, and do the summaries just mentioned.

No BS—it's all about respect. A false brand promise is worth less than no promise at all, just as one bad Starbucks experience can negate ten good ones. People expect performance. Gaining respect is an obvious part of building a brand, and it's amazing how BS is eventually sniffed out—and how fast it kills respect. Always be honest and willing to admit mistakes and show others you'll go out of your way to avoid making them.

Tip #7: Above All, Be a Leader

"Be a leader? But I'm not even a supervisor!"

Don't get confused—I'm not talking about job descriptions here. Every job, from corporate CEO to fruit picker in an orchard, has leadership opportunities. Leaders are the shining lights in any work group who not only accomplish their job, they make things better for the rest of their organization. And it's possible to put leadership skills to use in almost any situation.

Leadership is a complex system of communication, behavior, trust, and actual job performance that inspires others to follow and do better—not forces, but inspires (which is often the difference between a manager and a leader). If you have the charisma and respect of others, it almost doesn't matter if you're the supervisor—people will follow you because of your persona.

DON'T RELY ON POSITION ALONE

There are two recognized kinds of power in most organizations: position power and personal power. Position power comes from the organization chart, which says so-and-so has the authority to hire, fire, tell you what to do, and pay you for doing it. Personal power has nothing to do with the organization chart, but with the willingness of some to follow others. It's a huge difference. If you feel you're relying entirely on authority granted by the org chart, you might be vulnerable.

Why Is It Important?

Sooner or later, leaders are recognized, and many become managers. If management is observant at all, they will recognize leadership traits—at least those that lead employees in the right direction—and keep and grow the folks who have them. If they don't, you're probably working for the wrong organization anyway.

What to Do

Don't be all about yourself. Stay focused on the task and the organization, not on yourself. Nobody cares about your pay and benefits, and your sick kids are a subject for the break room, not the workplace floor. Empathy, the ability to see things through the eyes of others, is a core leadership skill; learn to view the world through the eyes of bosses and coworkers.

Take the right kinds of risks. Smart leaders take the right kinds of risks. They don't live in fear and cower in a corner doing nothing, but they don't say or do things that might risk the entire work group or enterprise, either. When people see you're smart about risk, that you'll take enough to get the job done but not so much that you rock the boat needlessly, you'll build trust.

Don't wait to be told what to do. Bosses (good ones, anyway) don't like employees who sit around waiting for orders; they like well-channeled initiative. Remember, part of your job is to make your boss's job easier.

Look for ways to expand your role. Most leaders are willing to put more on their plate because of their nature as leaders, and because they're good at moving mundane or unnecessary tasks to different places. Bosses see value in people who are willing to take on more work, but don't be the hotshot who takes on more work while letting the work you're supposed to do slide.

Tip #8: Build a Safety Net—Just in Case

Yes, the first seven tips showed you how to become indispensable, but what if you're "dispensed" anyway? You need a lifeboat or two, just in case.

Why Is It Important?

As I'll develop further in Chapter 4, "If the Ax Falls," your actions and behaviors once you're let go are critical to a successful return to your financial and career feet. Finding a new job or career is hard enough without worrying about where your next house payment or gallon of milk is going to come from. So it's important to build a reserve, one that can be tapped just to keep things going.

What to Do

Build an emergency fund. Everyone should have one. Financial advisers suggest three to six months of total expenses set aside in a liquid (always available) savings account. Don't keep the money in stocks, insurance policies, home equity, or something else you might have to sell, but in cash savings.

Find comparable resources. Of course, savings are the best. But the amount you need to save might be less if your family has a second income coming in (e.g., if your spouse works). Some families, younger ones in particular, may have helpful in-laws or other family help. The important thing is to know you can replace your income somehow.

. . . But don't take 401(k) loans. I don't usually recommend them anyway, because you give up any growth on the balance used for the loan. Worse, if you lose your job, your loan becomes due and payable—just when you don't need something like that to happen.

Begin taking off-the-top savings. The tried and true—and best—way to accumulate savings for an emergency fund, for a 401(k) loan payoff, or for any other goal is to have a fixed amount removed off the top of your paycheck. It's an automatic deposit to some form of savings account that you connect to your paycheck. The money never hits your checking account and you never see it. So as times get tough, the tough have enough discipline to squirrel away more nuts. A good goal is 5 to 10 percent of your check, but anything is better than nothing.

Chapter 2

Improving the Merchandise

The last chapter was aimed squarely at playing defense: How to keep your existing job and become more valuable, so when the big bosses come around looking for "volunteers" to get the ax, your name never makes it onto that list.

The old sports adage, "The best offense is a good defense" often carries the day in the workplace as well. To protect what you have, to make that shell or carapace a little more difficult to crack, is sometimes the best way not only to preserve your job but also to get ahead. Indeed, in many workplaces, the folks who get ahead are steady, never waste time, and never take risks or make mistakes.

But sometimes the reverse is true. The best defense can be a good offense, too. Stay a little ahead of the game and you'll not only be prepared to handle the bad stuff in any work environment, you'll be prepared to get out of its way. You'll also be better prepared to get the good stuff.

What do I mean? Well, in many industries, downsizing is simply an economic fact of life. Companies are engaging in a long-term drive to become more efficient, whether through the deployment of technology or the outsourcing and offshoring of jobs that can be done cheaper or more efficiently elsewhere. You cannot avoid this.

What you can do is see it coming. Like a flash flood, you can elevate or sidestep yourself onto higher ground. That doesn't stop the water, and it doesn't stop the water from flooding those downstream or unable to leave its path, but it does enable you to keep the high ground.

This chapter is about building both a depth and a breadth of knowledge in your current industry—or a new industry—not just by playing defense, but also by playing a little offense. The tips cover topics like improving skill sets and adding new competency to your career portfolio. They also cover marketing your skills—not just to your employer and others around you, but by creating recognition of you into a broader space in your industry or beyond it.

Tip #9: Sharpen the Saw

Stephen Covey used this phrase to great effect in his bestselling *Seven Habits of Highly Effective People*. It's the easiest to remember and possibly the most relevant of his seven habits. And further, you can do something about it.

Sharpening the saw means moving forward—or "up the value chain" as I saw it described once—to either make yourself more valuable in what you currently do or more valuable for what you might do someday—or both. No matter what you do, building skills and competencies is important. Change is real, and you need to keep up.

Why Is It Important?

Face it, as people get older or do one thing for a long time, they get set in their ways. It's human nature to do what works, and if it works that's okay, and if it ain't broke, why fix it? But such an attitude, while often sufficient, may leave you in the path of the flood described above.

Juliet Wehr Jones, attorney and CEO of Career Key, a career counseling company, puts it this way: "If you can feel confident you can do something well, you're more likely to do it and actually *do it* well." So sharpening the saw—the breadth and depth of your skill sets—is key not only to doing your job better, but also to making yourself more desirable to others who may hire you.

What to Do

Be your industry. Read outside press and industry trade materials, talk to people, do whatever you need to do to become an expert on the computer industry, chemical industry, health care, or whatever industry you work in. Not only do you become the go-to person described in Chapter 1, you can put this knowledge into play on your job. If you're interested in working in another industry, be that industry, too.

Take a skills inventory. Sure, you know how to prepare a daily report or close out a register or sterilize your lab equipment. That's great, and it pays to be the best you can be in those areas. But step outside of yourself and think of the bigger picture. What about project management? Customer service skills? Skills in dealing with people in other countries? Problem-solving skills? My corporate job gave me a wealth of project management skills translating perfectly into my current career as a writer and book author. I recommend listing all of your skills on a pad of paper, even if seemingly farfetched. Give examples. You'll be surprised how rich this exercise can be.

Watch others closely. You can only learn so much by reading or receiving training on the skill sets of your job. It helps to find someone in your organization—or some other organization—who does what you want to do or think you should be doing. Watch how they operate. Talk to them. The best way to learn is to learn by example.

Practice, practice, practice. As they say, practice makes perfect. If you're trying to deepen or broaden your skills, nothing works better than actually doing it. Be willing to volunteer or help others doing what you think you should be doing. Pay your dues. Get the experience. Learn from it.

Tip #10: Tap the Network

On average, people change jobs once every seven years or so, and that trend is accelerating. Time was, if you did change jobs, you did it through a formal process of searching for openings, sending a resume, and interviewing. That process, of course, still exists. But just as social networking makes it easier for you to get the scoop on your neighborhood or friends, career networking makes it much easier to keep hooked into what's going on in the career world.

Why Is It Important?

Career networking makes it easier to know what's going on in the industry, who's hiring and what skill sets they seek—in short, to be exposed to opportunities. It's also a way to sharpen skills, because networks will provide role models and technical and "soft" information you need to do your job. Put another way—without a network, you risk being left out.

What to Do

Join professional or trade associations. Not every job is aligned with a professional or trade association, but you'd be surprised how many are. Check out Peter Weddle's human resource portal, known as "Weddles"—specifically the association directory at *http://www.weddles.com/associations/index.cfm.* Join, go to meetings, read the materials, talk to others.

Attend trade shows. If you can get to an industry trade show, you'll be amazed at not only what you learn about the industry (for "Be your industry," in Tip #9) but also who you meet. Pay part, or all, of your way if you have to. You'll shake hands and get business cards from folks you never thought of. Every trade show I've been to has yielded a surprise.

Get "Linked In." The Internet has something for everyone, and yes, there's a site that helps you get and stay networked with others in your industry. Linked In (*www.linkedin.com*) is a giant electronic directory allowing you to post information about yourself, read it about others, and contact them. It's a place to seek employment as well. At the time of writing, it had 24 million members in 150 industries.

Be genuine. A big handshake and a hearty, "Nice to meet you." You've heard it before and thought you had a new friend in the industry—only to find out later you had nothing. Follow up. Be genuine, and others will be, too. Networking is important for all who are employed, but don't take up inordinate amounts of someone's time at a trade-group meeting or trade show. Be polite, and find ways you can help them, too.

Tip #11: Create an Industry Brand

Tip #6 explained how to build your own internal brand through a combination of establishing consistency and dependability in your work and doing a few simple things to bring attention to it. The idea here is the same, except the arena is the entire industry (or network, as defined above)—not just the organization you work for.

Why Is It Important?

Branding for a company like Apple means, when you think of the name, you think of qualities such as "cutting edge" and "great design." Branding for yourself builds trust and recognition among your peers, superiors, and even subordinates by giving them qualities to identify with you. Now, as it extends outside your four walls, it becomes more about conveying excellence among your peers to the extent you're a known excellent quantity elsewhere, doors open, people know who you are, they trust you, they're willing to talk to you, and of course, they want to hire you.

What to Do

Volunteer for leadership. I talked about professional and trade associations above, and one simple way to build your brand is to become its president or take another leadership position. It not only shows leadership skills and initiative, but also an easily recognized commitment and dedication to what you do. So, while becoming president of the local chapter of the American Academy of Actuaries might not sound like a path to fun, it will help.

Present at meetings and trade shows. Attend those trade shows, and circulate your name, image, and work, and you'll build your brand. Better yet, make a presentation or lead a seminar or workshop. Others will notice.

Write an article or a paper. Get yourself published in a trade-association rag and others will recognize not only your name, but also your expertise. Even better, write a book. There's lots of ways to do this without making an all-out commitment to writing, which you might not have time for. Find a coauthor or publishing partner to handle the heavy lifting. The important thing is to get your name on it. If slow times are making your work slow, writing a paper (with permission, of course) is a great way to advance your career while doing something useful with the time.

Get yourself written about. An article in the local paper, magazine, website, or the *Business Journal* can do wonders. It becomes part of your portfolio and persona forever. Find an angle, and get to know some of the local reporters. Remember—they're looking for stories, too, so you're not imposing if you have something to say (authorized by your employer, of course). This has worked for me—see *http://www.sacmag.com/media/Sacramento-Magazine/ November-2006/Personality-Peter-Sander/.*

Invent something. Writing a paper or presenting shows expertise, as does inventing or devising something new in the industry. Many organizations have rewards for patents, but even if they don't, if you have an idea, go for it (again, with management permission). If it flies, you'll be recognized in your organization, and if you present it right, you'll be seen outside, too.

Tip #12: Perfect Your Resume

Many people who are happy in their current jobs don't think much about resumes. But tough times are the best times to dust off these handy documents of our professional lives. Even if you don't plan to change jobs, it's nice to take inventory of who you are and what you've done. And if you find yourself suddenly in the job market, well, now you're prepared.

Why Is It Important?

You know you, and your friends and coworkers know you, but what do you look like as a standard "shelf item" in the career marketplace? A generic white box or a dynamic product of high caliber? Outside of an outstanding reputation or "brand" in your career space, a resume says more about you—especially in a first impression—than anything else. It's a package on your work "product," and you'd better have one if you're planning to sit on any store shelf.

What to Do

Get your resume in line with the times. The art of resume writing has greatly evolved with PCs and tools to prepare professional documents on your own. There are several formats you can use to document your life. And you should prepare several technical formats, too—text (to imbed in e-mail messages), rich-text format (RTF, for printed versions), and .pdf files (again for print, and to avoid virus-infection concerns for the recipient and to keep alignment and special fonts and characters intact).

Customize. Technology not only makes the perfect resume easier to format, it also allows you to easily customize resumes for different positions. Some versions can start with a career goal or objective, others could start with a personal profile—either of which can be adapted to the organization or job you're applying for. The personal profile sums up who you are, what you've done, what you're looking for, and character traits an employer or recruiter might be interested in—sort of a 30-second "elevator speech" about you. Create a core resume that includes all relevant pieces, and prepare it to add custom elements.

The latest and greatest. Of course, content is just as important, if not more so, than format. Take a careful inventory of your background and accomplishments. Have other coworkers, bosses, or even friends help. What may not seem important to you just might be to others.

Use the resources. As you might expect, there are plenty of resources to help you "imagineer" and construct your resume. Books include *Knock 'em Dead Resumes* (Martin Yate, Adams Media, 2008). Websites like Quintessential Careers (*www.quint careers.com*) and Resume Resource (*www.resume-resource.com*) give plenty of real-world advice. A Google search on "resume format" gives some handy image templates up front, plus plenty of references to others. Finally, job-search site Monster.com offers a handy "Resume Tips by Industry" in their "Career Tips and Advice" section (*http://career-advice.monster.com*).

Tip #13: Learn Who's Hiring and Why

In today's world the job market changes at a frightening pace. Faster economic cycles, shorter product life cycles, and frequent outsourcing mean constant change. If you're in the job market (and even if you aren't), it's important to follow your industry and other relevant ones to see where the job "puck" is going.

Why Is It Important?

You're a seller—of your services to an organization. The trick is, of course, to find buyers. To market yourself most effectively, it helps to place yourself square in front of the largest group of buyers. For that matter, knowing where the buyers are will also help you customize your product (your skill set) and marketing (your resume and other efforts to gain visibility).

What to Do

Read job reports. Reading—and keeping current—is really important. The U.S. Bureau of Labor Statistics publishes several monthly job reports, including the Job Openings and Labor Turnover survey. (Go to *www.bls.gov/jlt* and follow links under "Economic News Releases.") BLS reports give the national picture, and in a downturn, your local newspaper or website has plenty of "ink" on the local situation. Read the business pages regularly.

Tap the network. There's no time like crunch time to tap your networks to find out who's hiring and for what. So before the speeches start and while you're eating lunch at that Toastmasters meeting, ask your neighbor if his company is hiring. Ask your neighbors at home, too, for that matter. And at those professional association meetings. You get the idea.

Watch job sites. The Internet makes digging so much easier than ten or fifteen years ago. Sites like CareerBuilder show sorted lists by job categories, cities, and companies. Make a habit of looking at individual company or public agency sites on a regular basis, too. It's a good thing to do for an hour or so, say, every Sunday night.

Other resources. Finding the gold among all those rocks naturally requires creativity and resourcefulness. Again, use trade associations, magazines, websites, and similar resources. Make some contacts at the national headquarters of the trade association you're part of. College alumni associations are building effective networking sites and programs. And on the local front, read the local edition of the *Business Journal* regularly if available.

Tip #14: Toward a New Career

You've thought about it long and hard. The industry's going nowhere, or the business you work in just isn't cutting it. Market is shrinking, too many players, new technology, moving off-shore—there are a million possible reasons over which you have no control. Rather than waiting for the ax to fall, you want to reinvent yourself now. Play offense and be proactive. How?

Why Is It Important?

Nothing lasts forever. In fact, today's careers are shorter than ever—or should I say, have more stops, where you need to get off and travel another route. So in good times or bad, but especially bad, you need to consider what else is out there. It isn't so much a "grass is greener" proposition but rather one of finding high ground when the floodwaters rise. It's a good habit, too, because maximizing your career potential during good times is also important. Or maybe it's just time for a change.

What to Do

Take someone else's inventory. Finding a role model is a good way to start on another career. Network your way to someone already doing what you'd like to do. Spend time with him or her. Buy lunch. Offer to help. Ask lots of questions, take inventory of what he or she's doing and how he or she got there. What skills, what formal training, what on-the-job training was needed?

Make a plan. The saying, "If you fail to plan, you plan to fail" is true for career change. I've seen many take short, unprepared stabs at doing something new only to get repulsed and lose confidence necessary for the next try. A career action plan is like a business plan: What's the market? What's the product? What's necessary to get the product to market? Your plan should cover specific facets of the new career, how you do and don't fit, and what you need for a better fit.

Get the hard skills. Part of the plan, of course, is to acquire any specific skills necessary to do the job. Be prepared to spend the time (and money) to train or volunteer. Spend plenty of "sponge" time among trade associations and with individuals in the industry.

Get the soft skills. Many career-change candidates stop with the hard skills—if they go that far at all. Make sure your plan covers time to see how things really work on the job. What's a work day like? What kinds of resources do you need, and what do you have? Use your network to learn soft skills, and use your quest for soft skills to build your network.

Tip #15: Get a Pedigree

You check for "MD" when you see a doctor or "DDS" or "DMD" when you see a dentist. Or for any specialist for that matter—if someone has a credential or a degree in the field, it shows knowledge, commitment, and that they've paid their dues. And no, you don't have to go through ten years of medical training to get a credential—some can be had in a matter of weeks. But—fair warning—many credentials are fabrications of the institutions that may grant them—and take your money. Be selective, buyer beware.

Why Is It Important?

A credential becomes part of your personal brand and a badge of achievement in the field. It is also something that translates well from one organization to another. Every organization might do business differently, but get a PMP—Project Management Professional—credential, and it shows you've met the basic requirements to be a project manager in most organizations.

What to Do

Research three- and four-letter credentials. There are hundreds. The Financial Industry Regulatory Authority tallies eighty-six known credentials in the financial advisory space alone (*http://apps.finra.org/ datadirectory/1/prodesignations.aspx*). The best way to find them is through trade groups or knowledgeable individuals in the industry.

Decide which are best. Now comes the hard part. Check out the requirements and see what the trade press has to say about worthwhile and worthless designations. A broader credential (like a CFP®or Certified Financial Planner) may mean more than a CEBS or Certified Employment Benefits Specialist—unless that's specifically what you want to do.

Consider other benefits. Getting your credential puts you into a pool of like-minded individuals working in like professions, so it becomes a great opportunity to build your network.

Don't spend more than it's worth. Like most life decisions, it's a cost/benefit tradeoff. How much time and money will you spend getting the credential, and will the credential really get you what you want? Talk to the providers, but also to other practitioners in the industry. Ask if your company will help pay for classes that pertain to your job.

Tip #16: Don't Forget about Recruiters

There are people and entire businesses whose role in life is to find you a job. Well, not completely, but that's the effect. Executive recruiters (headhunters) are typically hired by companies looking to fill positions. That said, you can approach them (most of them, anyway) for a job, because after all, people is what they're looking for. Recruiters operate mostly at the professional level—skilled white-collar jobs like engineering and management—while employment agencies fill operative positions.

Why Is It Important?

Recruiters have knowledge of existing positions and can help you market yourself to achieve these positions. Since recruiters are typically hired and paid by the hiring organization, they're mostly interested in you if you're a well-qualified, high-performing, top-tier candidate. But they make money placing people, so don't give up even if you're inexperienced or a midrange employee. Again, they can often point you in a useful direction, even if they can't place you in a job at the moment.

What to Do

Learn the types of recruiters. Retained search firms work mostly at the highest level of management, and they get paid regardless of whether a candidate is found. They generally know who's who and whom they want to target for a position, so if your phone isn't ringing already, you're probably not one of their targets. Contingency firms, on the other hand, only get paid if someone is hired and are more often used in the middle-management and skill ranks. As an individual, you can approach a contingency firm. If they think you could be a match for something, they'll work with you.

Get on the radar. Use branding techniques to gain visibility, in addition to an exemplary resume. Recruiters have a lot of doors they can get you through, but can only get you through those doors if you're a pretty good product.

Know when to use recruiters—and when not to. Recruiters work best when the type of work you do, and the level at which you do it, are in high demand. But they're there to make money, and if that means placing you in a midrange job, they'll do it—especially in tough times when the job market is contracting. They need to eat, too. Be warned that working with a recruiter can be frustrating and difficult, because in most cases, someone else is paying them, not you.

A BIG RED BOOK

There are organizations for everything, and an organization called Kennedy Information Services keeps track of and publishes information for the hundreds of recruiters around the country. Look for the big red Directory of Executive Recruiters, published each year, at their website (*www.kennedyinfo.com*) or at a bookstore or library. Or their *Pocket Guide to Working with Executive Recruiters* which, full disclosure, I put together for them a few years ago.

Tip #17: Use the Internet to Expand Your Search

As the saying goes: "On the Internet, they don't know you're a dog!" The Internet has facilitated the match between employers and prospective employees with the advent of job databases, search engines, and even more advanced features to connect A to B. Huge general job-search sites have evolved just to make these matches, with lots of tools and upgrades to make the task of making contact easier and more targeted and real time. The downside, however, is that the ease of making contact has saddled employers with hundreds, thousands, even millions of responses, so getting through the fog has itself become a big issue.

Why Is It Important?

The Internet connects you to a very wide world, and the speed of contact and response is greatly enhanced. If you don't use the Internet, someone might question how up to date you really are. Even if you don't use the Internet to make contact, it's still one of the best ways to see what's out there. Finally, you can conduct your job search from pretty much anywhere you can set up a laptop and get online.

What to Do

Know the best sites. The three general sites are Monster (*www .monster.com*), Hotjobs (*http://hotjobs.yahoo.com*), and Career-Builder.com (*www.careerbuilder.com*). These sites offer highly evolved search tools, allowing you to pinpoint the job, company, location, and "flavor" of the job—not just "editing/writing" but "technical writing" or "digital content development" or "proofreading." Beyond the general sites, industry-specific sites like Dice (*www.dice.com*) for tech jobs or EFinancialCareers (*www.efinancial jobs.com*) for government jobs can help. Finally, don't forget professional and trade association sites—many contain member job postings.

Develop strategies. Search and find works best, and for you techie types, various "bots" are available to search and notify you of openings. Experts differ on how and how often to send resumes. As mentioned earlier, while automation helps, it has also clogged the system. So I recommend targeting your resumes carefully, sending when you only really mean to apply, and going outside the website occasionally (some companies make it impossible to do this) so your resume arrives in a separate electronic or even physical "pile." Of course, finding an internal contact through your network, once you've identified the position, helps immensely. That brings up a final point—don't abandon your traditional job-search strategies just to do the Internet search. Networking—the human kind—still works best.

Do this only at home, please. Your job may be on the line, but it's still bad form in most situations to sit around doing a job search on company time and using company resources. Unless, of course, you've been given an unsolicited green light by management; when that happens, you know it's time to find another job.

Chapter 3

The Other Side of the Fence

You want to keep your job, but maybe the writing is on the wall and it's time to do something else, anyway. You know—that business idea you always talk and dream of when you're on vacation. The one you think about in the shower, while sitting in rush-hour traffic, while your kids kick the soccer ball around.

It never hurts to think about such a thing. In fact, as corporations downsize they constantly think about what they can hire out to people like you. Business startups—including freelancer self-employed types—are at an all-time high. Where once it was thought to be heresy to switch corporate jobs, now it's considered fashionable to venture out on your own. In fact, it can work in your favor. Why? Well, when management realizes you have an alternative—that they're competing with you for your services—your value just might rise in their eyes. Sure, some old-school bosses will let you go at the first hint dropped of jumping ship, but more and more today, bosses may applaud your initiative and may even help you get started. If they don't, you might be working in the wrong place anyway.

But Is This the Time?

Now you might ask, why even think about starting a business when the economy sucks? Great question. Yes, there are some challenges, and depending on the industry, they can be severe. It just doesn't make sense to start a construction business during a real-estate downturn. When the economy is bad, there's less to go 'round for everyone. However, a business that helps other businesses perform more cheaply and efficiently can be "spot on" when things are bleak.

When the economy sucks, companies, like you and me as individuals, look especially hard for ways to tighten the ol' belt. And that might put your job in jeopardy, but it also forces clear thinking about what they want to do in-house versus farm out to others —like human resources services, payroll, or building a website. Downsizing—or rightsizing—can make it the time to start a business that sells certain services or products to larger organizations.

And keep in mind, as a new business owner, you'll have lots of startup costs, lots of things to buy. They'll be cheaper and easier to find, as you'll find it a "buyer's market" for rent, equipment, supplies, even the folks you want to hire. So lean times aren't necessarily the wrong times; in fact, they can be quite right. It just means you need to be smart and plan carefully. And you need to recognize that if your business idea involves a high-end restaurant or something else that thrives on a good economy, there might be a better time to act. But that doesn't mean this isn't the time to work on your plans.

Greener Grass Doesn't Always Taste Good

Starting a business involves risks—it would be irresponsible to say otherwise. Many small businesses fail. More die of poor planning than almost anything else. So your remaining time on the job is vitally important in the formative stages of any business, because the bills are still getting paid and the family is happy. Starting to think about a business while still employed greatly reduces the risk—as does starting the business itself, if you do it right.

Many folks just aren't cut out for entrepreneurship. The grass looks greener on the other side, sure, but they can never really get there, and thinking about that green grass merely becomes a hindrance and distraction. I can't tell you whether you have what it takes or whether you should head toward that greener pasture. But it's a good exercise to think about it, whether you end up doing it or not. Even if you don't end up starting a business, the entrepreneurial thought process can make you more effective in your current job.

Tip #18: Find What Speaks to You

Here's the beaten-to-death question asked by anyone bitten by the entrepreneurial bug: "What kind of business should I start?"

It's really tough. There's a big difference between a good idea and a good business. And the last thing you want to do is invest big—financially and emotionally—in a good idea that turns out to be a bad business. You want a good business, one that you have a passion for, one to which you bring unique skills and talents few others have.

Why Is It Important?

Finding the right business involves finding a good idea for the marketplace and getting the fundamentals and mechanics right. But there's one more thing to consider: you. You're the driver and the glue that holds the business together. It's your background and skill set that makes the difference; otherwise, you're just a passive investor. So, it's important to find something you can completely connect with.

What to Do

Take a skills inventory. Sound familiar? Probably so, if you read the last two chapters on preserving and expanding your job horizons. Here it is again, but with an eye toward going out on your own. What can you do? What job skills do you have that can be sold to others? Used in a small business? Project management skills? Negotiating skills? Writing or speaking skills? Creative talents? A long list, probably. Write them all down; then review them with colleagues and friends because they will see things you don't see.

Pick out the unique ones. Some among those listed skills will be unique. Negotiating contracts with offshore businesses? Maybe you should start an import-export business. Preparing marketing or business plans? Become a professional grant writer. You get the idea.

Start here: what does your company need? You may be planning—dreaming of—your getaway, cold turkey, gone. But where you are is one of the best places to start in thinking about a business. What services does your company need, and would it make sense to buy them from someone like you? You have the skills already. It could be a smooth win-win transition, and oh-by-the-way, you could perform similar services for others. It doesn't always work—but it's a place to start.

Leave no ideas behind. I'm big on assembling lists, because lists get you to think outside the box. Sure, you'll end up with a lot of dumb ideas, but getting them all out on the table requires the necessary thought process. So keep a running log of all your business ideas. You don't have to develop all of them—just the few good ones that bubble to the top.

Assemble a review committee. Especially when times are tough, there's a tendency not to think clearly. Emotions swirl, the grass is greener, this has gotta work, that can never work, etc., etc.; it's human nature. So build a little network to bounce ideas off of— colleagues, family, friends, or other acquaintances in the field you might be trying to get into.

Tip #19: Niche and Get Rich

Full disclosure: Along with my wife Jennifer, I wrote a book by this title (*Niche and Get Rich*, Entrepreneur Press, 2003). Why? Because she and I saw, over and over, the same mistake made by hundreds of would-be entrepreneurs.

What's the mistake? It's starting a me-too business. Yet another business selling a traditional retail product in a retail storefront to the public at large. Yet another garden café at yet another street corner along the same boulevard. What's wrong with this picture? It's this: You can't compete with Wal-Mart or Applebee's or the other regional or national giants that dominate the space. You need to find a niche. A unique, defensible, small-but-profitable part of the market not being served by the Big boys.

Why Is It Important?

The Wal-Marts and Applebee's of the world have resources. Resources to advertise, discount, and flood the floor with loss leaders (that is, products that aren't designed to make a profit but are intended to get traffic into the store) to get traffic. Traffic that's only as loyal to them as the most recent glossy ad or discounted price. So they have to do it over and over. You can't afford to do this.

What to Do

Don't just look for markets—find niche markets. Get this right from the beginning: You don't want to market to everyone. You can't afford it, and everyone else is trying to do it. What you're looking for is a small but definable group underserved by what's currently out there. Left-handed people. People or businesses where having something delivered or making a house call makes a difference.

Define a niche product. A product or service can be differentiated physically (left-handed scissors) or by a level of service (professional-quality brochures delivered overnight). It can be differentiated by distribution (a website that sells unicycles nationally like unicycle.com) or by location (make and sell smoothies down at the beach). The possibilities are endless once you start thinking about them. And I recommend the book.

Test your ideas. The trick is to find a niche market that's big enough and loyal enough to be served by your business. That's where developing and testing your ideas comes into play. Try your ideas out with friends and potential customers in the niche market. If there are enough of them, and the response is genuinely positive, you might be on to something. And always be prepared to refine your ideas.

Tip #20: Take This Piggy to Market

For many folks, the word "marketing" gets mixed up with advertising, and when thinking about marketing, they think about how to generate hype and hoopla through glossy ads. Well, that's only part of the story, a part that may or may not emerge from a well-thought-out marketing plan.

Why Is It Important?

No business can succeed in a vacuum. It must have customers. It must have a product or service that connects with customers. It must be able to sell those services often enough at a high-enough price to make a profit. Marketing is the "sizzle on the steak" and the package on the product, but it also means a good enough knowledge of customers and customer habits to make the connection.

What to Do

Learn all you can about the market. It's the same set of questions you've probably asked or heard asked in your workplace. Who are your customers? What do they want? Are we giving them what they want? Do they know we can give them what they want? Successful entrepreneurs ask these questions and go to great lengths to learn everything they can about the size and needs of a market. And always think about what will make a market grow. That's especially important in a weak economy, which is unforgiving toward small businesses with poor plans.

Take a trip to the idea factory. Now the lid comes off, and it's time to think outside the box. What's the right marketing strategy? How should you price your products? Add special charges for delivery? What kinds of alliances or cobranding or colocating strategies might work? Should you do business on the Internet? How?

Brand and name your business. This part is even more fun. What should you call yourself? What should you call your products? "L'eggs" in the 1970s was one of the cleverest names in history—catchy, descriptive of both product and package, and it differentiated a dull, mundane product. Names aren't just for fun; they have a lot to do with the greater marketing strategy you have in mind. L'eggs wasn't just about putting hosiery in the store, it was about creating attention on the shelf, which motivated the retailer to stock it. But you can certainly start with names and brands and circle back once your marketing plan is clearer.

Tip #21: Run the Numbers

At some point, you have to get real and run some numbers. Convert those sales into dollars and put some dollar figures on production costs and overhead.

Why Is It Important?

More businesses fail due to lack of funding than any other cause, and you need a plan to think through the funding before you start. And that thing about the difference between a good idea and a good business—here's where the rubber meets the road.

What to Do

Start with startup costs. So maybe a PC, an Internet connection, and a printer are all you need, along with a small unused corner of your home. Great—what could be better—little to no startup cost, especially if you already have these things. Maybe it's a restaurant with a $400,000 kitchen and numerous budget-breaking cosmetic changes to get going. Whatever; you need to cost it out realistically. If the nut is too big to crack, find something else to do. When transitioning from employment, starting a business with low-to-no startup costs is best.

Estimate price, cost, operating expenses. Figure out the flow-through in your business—how much you'll sell, how much it will cost to produce, and all of those other expenses associated with operating your business. It's too big to detail here, but a computer spreadsheet and some digging into the cost figures are the two places to start.

Do the what-if. Once you've built your basic business model, it's time to do what all those high-priced consultants do in the business space—"scenario planning." Try your numbers with low, medium, and high sales assumptions; low, medium, and high cost assumptions. Is your business bulletproof? Or does just one best-case scenario allow survival. Bravo if you come up green in most scenarios.

Not just business finances—review personal finances, too. Most entrepreneurs focus on their business. They get it right. Meanwhile, their personal finances fall apart. And if the business has strong connections to the personal finances (which is normal in the beginning, but a bad idea long term), it gets ugly. A good business plan should go hand in hand with a good personal financial plan. For more on this topic, see another of my books: *The Ultimate Guide to Personal Finance for Entrepreneurs* (Entrepreneur Press, 2007).

Tip #22: Build the Business Plan

A business plan? Just what you want to do when times are tough and you're all stressed out—write a document. Yuck.

Sure, it's nice to have a document neatly prepared with pictures in a color-coordinated binder with your name on it. It'll help with bankers, suppliers, and perhaps the in-laws that might be writing a check to get you started. But focus on the document itself, and you miss the point. It's about getting you to think your business through, and about clarity.

A good business plan addresses the market, the product or service, and everything you have to do to bring that product or service to market. It addresses phases of the business, capital, legal, personnel, and a laundry list of other requirements.

Why Is It Important?

Without a business plan, you may neglect important aspects or characteristics of your business. It's natural to focus on what you're good at or comfortable with and leave the nitty-gritty—like working capital requirements or licensing—for later. Sure, you have good instincts, but instincts aren't complete and may be hard to communicate to others. A business plan helps address the issues in a balanced way and communicate to others. Remember, a business plan isn't a contract—it doesn't lock you into anything—it's a template to organize your thoughts.

What to Do

Put it all together. There are a lot of ways to organize a business plan. At its core, there should be a marketing plan, an operating plan, and a financing plan. There are plenty of good business planning books; one is *The Successful Business Plan* by Rhonda Abrams.

SWOT it out. The SWOT—Strengths, Weaknesses, Opportunities, Threats—grid is a handy way to analyze your business idea. Fill the grid in; it's interesting, and helps point you to issues that need to be addressed in the business plan.

Test it out. Once you sketch out the business plan, show it to others. See if it makes sense. See if anything's missing. There's a world full of free consultants out there—take advantage.

Check in with a small biz consultant. As workplaces have shrunk, a number of folks have set up shop as consultants or "growth coaches" for small businesses. Before you take the plunge, it's worth a short review.

Keep modifying it! A business plan is a living document. As you eat, sleep, drive, and work you'll keep thinking of new ideas, and others will supply them for you. And remember, a business plan doesn't have to be perfect, it just has to be good, and it needs to adapt to good times and bad.

Tip #23: Keep a Foot in Both Camps

So you're gonna just get up one Friday afternoon, walk out the door, and start your new business? Think again. You'll be in an emotional tizzy. You won't have any money. You'll fret every minute of every day about making your first dime. Is that the way to get started?

In a word, no. The preparation process should start as long as possible before your work assignment ends—either voluntarily or involuntarily. Yes, that means you probably should *always* be working on your business idea! And to the extent possible, you should start your business—even if only on a small scale—while still employed.

Why Is It Important?

It's important to hit the ground running. With some momentum, some experience, and hopefully, with some cash flow. It simply works better. I started my writing career a year and a half before I left my high-tech job, and it was a blessing. Also, if you start sooner, you'll get the experience and leave some of those newcomer mistakes long behind before you become dependent on your business.

What to Do

Make a firm commitment—with your family. Get everyone behind you, and hopefully, in a position to help you. Sure, working a full-time job plus noodling around in your business is going to take time away from family activities. It's going to be stressful. Without a family commitment, it will assuredly be a lot more stressful.

Look for ways to test drive your business. Figure out how to do your business out of your home or possibly in partnership with someone else already in the business. Work for someone else, even for free, for a while. As an early writer, I found others to partner with on projects and set aside periods of time during my home life—mostly in the early morning or after young children were in bed. And make sure to avoid potential conflicts of interest—if your day job is software engineering, it's bad form to do software development for a competitor on the side.

What and when to tell your boss. This is tricky, and it depends a bit on your situation and your boss. I prefer the upfront, candid approach—over time, it builds trust and credibility—and I've seen the boss actually take an interest and help at times. You don't want your boss to find out through some other channel, especially if your side business is causing any drag whatsoever on your day job.

And it's bad form to use the company copy machine, etc., to run your business. You'll know when it's time—but the earlier the better.

Tip #24: Don't Be Afraid to Ask

I have a good friend, a professional photographer, who was working for a large photofinisher with a separate studio as a side business. As an "outlier" to the core business, he was dissatisfied with most aspects of his job. So he decided to go out on his own. Loose business plan, $50,000 in capital equipment to buy, and start from scratch to build a clientele. Not very appealing.

But he did it anyway. He got the nerve and the cash and marched into the owner's office. Nervous but trying to be as confident as possible, he declared, "I'm leaving to start my own studio." His boss responded, "Hmmm, Dave, sit down. You know, I've been thinking about selling this studio. Would you like to buy it? I'll even finance it for you."

Why Is It Important?

The point of this story is pretty easy to see—it never hurts to ask. There might just be a surprise waiting for you out there, a win-win you may never have thought of, especially as big organizations work to get smaller.

What to Do

Get the ducks lined up behind you. If you're going to talk to someone important, it's important to know what you're doing. This is where preparation and having that business plan in your brain will help. Business owners and leaders see that you've done your homework and know your stuff and that you're serious. You might get the help you need—or even their business. If nothing else, you'll get their respect.

Think win-win. A positive energy and mode of thinking helps everywhere in life. When leaving to start a business, you should think about the win-win whenever possible, and strive for it. Find a way, in your new business, that you can help your old organization. If nothing else, be positive and complimentary to your old boss. You never know where you might cross paths again.

Don't start from scratch if you don't have to. As in the photo studio example, ask the right question at the right time, and you just may end up not having to start from scratch. That's huge.

Tip #25: Get Ready, Get Set, Bail

It's time to get started, time to formulate a graceful exit from your place of work, time to gain your feet slowly but surely toward happily ever after. You need a startup plan.

Why Is It Important?

If you don't plan the transition effectively, an awful lot can go wrong. Your business can get off on the wrong foot. You can leave your job on bad terms or before you had enough resources to get your business started and get by on the home front. The bad nightmare of a sucky economy might just get worse.

What to Do

Have an exit strategy. Before you actually do it, envision what life will be like on work's last day and Business Day One. Will you be ready to leave your job gracefully and in such a way that you don't alienate (or further alienate) your employer? Will you have identified or even helped to train your successor? Will your business be ready? Capital lined up? Savings set aside to buy groceries? You should jot down a script of what things will be like on that day, and work toward it in advance.

Launch day. Part of the script will include getting your business off the ground; finding the place, getting the employees, and telling the world that you exist. Do a plan for that, too.

Just in case. It's also good to do a contingency plan, just in case things don't work out as you expect them to. What would you do next? Are your doors still open at your previous employer? Are there other employers or work situations out there you could approach? Can you adapt your new business quickly to meet a market need? Building skills and building new avenues for the future hardly stop when you go out on your own. There are always greener pastures.

Chapter 4

If the Ax Falls

Monday morning: You listen to the news, brew some coffee, take a shower, and enjoy a quick croissant with the paper. Bad news all over—credit crunch, more job losses, another bank facing bankruptcy. Not a lot to get excited about. The fourth place finisher in the latest golf tournament made $200,000 playing four rounds of golf. How you wish you could have done that.

After the usual half hour in slow-and-go traffic, you wander into the office. A white envelope with your name on it has been placed on your keyboard. Nervously, you open it. It asks you to join a meeting with all employees in the Cabernet room at 9:00 A.M. You fiddle with e-mail and straighten a few things on your desk, but your heart isn't really into the morning.

The meeting happens. You walk in. Silence, mostly, with a few nervous laughs. Immediately, you notice the boss, with an HR rep, seated behind a table in the front of the room. Piled high in front of them are dozens of sealed, large-white envelopes.

Everyone sits down. "Good morning. You've all worked hard to make this company a success. But as you know, times have changed. It's tough out there, and we've had to make some difficult choices. Unfortunately, we've decided to close this office. The envelopes we're about to distribute contain information you'll need to move forward. Our HR reps will help you as much as possible. I can't say this enough—we didn't want to do this, and we hope for the best future for you and your families. If there's anything I can do, please don't hesitate to ask."

Stunned silence. You stare straight ahead. A few around you clear their throats. One of your more intrepid colleagues finally stands up and heads for the door; you and the rest follow gingerly.

Today's the first day of the rest of your life. Your best efforts and strongest hopes didn't stem the tide. Now what?

Well, your ship has taken a torpedo. You're feeling exposed, vulnerable, tentative. A real blow. But it's still important to do the right thing to keep the ship afloat and minimize the casualties— sail back into port, get another ship, and charge forward. That's what this chapter's about.

Tip #26: Don't Panic—Use the Safety Net

When the ax falls, panic is usually the first thing to set in. Well, maybe a few of those grief cycle things, too—denial, anger, depression. But panic is the one you need to worry about.

Sure, life will be different with much less or even no income. And now, the uphill battle of finding another job, too. And a family with kids who might not even understand what you're going through. And neighbors. And in-laws. Why me?

Why Is It Important?

Panic causes rash decisions: sell this, take that job right now. Heck, people even get divorced over job losses. It happens. A lot. But people will support you more than you think. There are safety nets to get you through the darkest hour. This, too, can be managed, and the skills and competence you used on the job will pull you through. Take the right attitude and use your skills and other assets to the fullest.

What to Do

Review your savings. Hopefully, you've accumulated an emergency fund (see Tip #8) of at least a few months' savings (financial advisers recommend three to six months' living expenses in savings). This is what it's for. That doesn't mean spend lavishly, but, wisely spent, these savings will give you the bridge to get to the other side. Warning: Avoid using retirement funds if at all possible.

Think about your spouse's income and benefits. Sure, as a family unit, you won't be making what you did before. You'll need a new income plan to get you by the next few months, that's obvious. But you should also—if you haven't already—take a look into your spouse's benefits, too. Yours might have been better, but his or hers are better than nothing.

Make an expense reduction plan. You and you as a family will have to tighten belts. That means looking at everything. Nothing is sacred. Sure, some costs, like your mortgage or rent payment, are more fixed than others, but a few months without cable TV, a 65°F house, and restaurant dinners won't hurt if it reduces your cash drain. Sit down with your family and go through it all.

File for unemployment. You've never collected it, and you thought it was only for "poor" folks. Not so. By law, your employer pays into a fund to finance your unemployment should it ever occur. It's yours, subject to certain rules, like time of service and reason you were let go. More than likely, your company will help you through the filing process. The process and benefits vary slightly by state, but the CareerOneStop Service Locator, sponsored by the U.S. Department of Labor, at *http://www.service locator.org/OWSLinks.asp* will get you started. You should also know that a new Federal law just put into place in July 2008 extends the benefit period by thirteen weeks beyond what your state allows, which is typically 26 weeks.

Know low-income options, if applicable. Like unemployment, the idea of collecting welfare may never have crossed your mind. But depending on your income and needs (children, other assets, etc.), you just might be eligible. Food stamps, low-cost health-care options, housing subsidies—it's worth swallowing your pride and checking them out with your local welfare or assistance office. Like unemployment insurance, you've probably earned it.

UNEMPLOYMENT BENEFITS: KNOW BEFORE YOU GO

As part of your preparation for the worst, it doesn't hurt to check out your state's unemployment benefits site to calculate your benefits in advance. It'll help you plan for what you need to save, and it may make you feel better about all those Federal and state programs you and/or other family members may have railed against from time to time.

Tip #27: Befriend a COBRA

For better or for worse, it's called the Consolidated Omnibus Budget Reconciliation Act, and it was passed back in 1986. It gives you the ability and right to continue health benefits provided by their group health plan under certain well-documented circumstances—which more likely apply than not. For a more complete description, see *http://www.dol.gov/dol/topic/health-plans/cobra.htm.*

That's the good news. The bad news is that you'll have to pay for all your health insurance. But it helps. Extending coverage is one of the first things you should do with your HR department, if you have one. If you work for a company with fewer than twenty employees, COBRA coverage isn't required.

Why Is It Important?

Keeping your insurance alive through COBRA not only keeps your family insured during your job transition, it also makes it far easier to get new insurance when you take your next career step.

What to Do

Not cheap, but you have other things to worry about. You'll probably be shocked at the COBRA insurance bill. In most cases, it's the easiest and cheapest way to go for full coverage similar to what you had before. You'll also find out how much your employer was paying to cover you. As suggested, you do have other things to worry about, and extending coverage through COBRA takes one biggie—health insurance—off the list.

Shop around, but . . . . It may pay to shop; you may be able to find cheaper, downsized, high-deductible coverage. But be aware that it can be quite difficult to increase your coverage once downsized. If you're planning to start a business or go out on your own, you'll likely end up with high-deductible coverage anyway, so now might be the time to shop.

Remember the high price of no insurance. Again, worth repeating: No insurance means no coverage; but worse, insurers hate coverage gaps and are less likely to cover you or cover at reasonable rates if they see uncovered periods.

Tip #28: Do Something, Anything

Your new role as "unemployed" can be quite discomfiting. You're perplexed, concerned about your future, maybe even a little embarrassed. You're concerned about what others might think about you—inside and outside the workplace. You want to withdraw, to suffer in silence, to hope no one sees you until you make a miraculous recovery into the working world.

It's all natural, but I suggest a different course. Take on some other form of work—even if a half-dozen notches below your professional stature—to keep things going and stay sharp.

Why Is It Important?

I once worked as a retail clerk and stockroom attendant for a high-end home furnishings and accessory retailer. It provided some income—not much, but some—and it gave me a chance to network, keep certain job skills sharp, and learn new skills in a new industry. I can run a cash register now. I learned new ways to talk to customers, I know more about retail, and that could help in my next job as many companies sell through retail. I built a new network. The employee discount was nice, especially at gift-giving time. No, it wasn't a career move, but it helped bridge a gap in a positive, constructive way.

What to Do

Get some income. Sure, $10 an hour won't get you by for long, but it helps, and in your current situation is likely to be tax free. And you don't have to settle for $10—there are lots of temporary higher-level positions available. I've also had good luck getting an assortment of jobs with temp agencies in my preprofessional past.

Yes, they'll understand. Sure, it'll feel odd at times when your colleagues see you stocking store shelves. Don't get caught up in the image game—this is all about you landing on your feet. People understand; in fact, they might even admire your flexibility and versatility. You can run a company and make a pretty mean latte, too!

Don't fall into the resume gap. For future employers, there's no bigger turnoff than finding big gaps in your resume. What did you do during that nineteen months you were laid off? Any kind of job or saw-sharpening exercise or significant project, like writing a book, is preferred to staying home tending the garden. You don't have to do it full time, but do something.

Discover something new! My time in retail gave me unique opportunities to have casual conversations with business owners, CEOs, CFOs, and their spouses as I loaded their cars or described the features of a living room lamp. They could see I wasn't a career stockboy and had more going for me, and it led to several conversations of interest and exchanges of business cards. And of course, I could have pursued advancement in the retail space if I had so chosen. It all spells "network opportunity."

Tip #29: Keep Your Attitude Up

It's easy to sink into a circle of despair when your job or business goes away: "I'm washed up," "They don't need me anymore," "Others out there who are younger or in some third-world country can do what I do." Your ego tracks your bank account downward.

As the saying goes, when it rains lemons, make lemonade. Turning "problem" and "challenge" into "opportunity" is the right way to think about it. It's your chance—your "license"—to do something new, to spread your wings, to step forward.

Why Is It Important?

Negative attitudes lead to negative work and negative impressions, and they lead to reluctance to pursue the things you could pursue. My departure from the corporate world was voluntary, but it gave me a real chance to become a researcher, writer, and book author, and I took it. The right attitude will open doors and make you more likely to go through them successfully.

What to Do

It's a job, not your career, and not your life. No doubt, unemployment should be taken seriously, but it isn't the end of your life. Especially in today's economy and employment norm, it's an understood step to something else. Again, it helps to think about it as an opportunity.

Be positive. No matter how well you think you control your emotions, a negative attitude will bleed through, if not in what you say or show, in what you do. When you're positive, you're confident, and when you're confident, it shows. Confidence will make subsequent employers far more likely to take you on.

Don't sweat the small stuff. When you're stressed, it's natural to get emotional and temperamental at the slightest stimulus. Forgot to attach that file? Damn! Car doesn't start on the first try? Now what?! Unemployment is a time to channel your energies into something positive, so as much as possible, keep the small stuff in the background.

Rely on your best friend. It's human nature—misery loves company, companionship helps through times of duress. You have a best friend somewhere: a spouse, an old school buddy, a work buddy. It's nice to have someone to test your latest news and ideas on, and the dialog will help you see new information clearly and position yourself more effectively. It sounds existential, but you are what others perceive you to be, and having someone to test that perception on is important.

Tip #30: Notify Creditors

It's natural to put your situation on ignore and hope it will go away. Ignore your finances, ignore your debt, ignore your investments, and try to keep a smile on your face; in fact, it's tempting to crawl into a shell and not notify anyone when you become unemployed. Especially a creditor who might sock you with an immediate payment demand and ding your credit report.

But most experts suggest being up front and proactive with creditors, notifying them in writing of your new status.

Why Is It Important?

The Consumer Credit Counseling Service (*www.cccsinc.org*) points out that the main objective of creditors, of course, is to get repaid. So if you're having trouble, most would like to know, and in some cases they will help out by rescheduling payments until you find new employment. Even if they don't, it never hurts to ask.

What to Do

Make a list. Make a list of all creditors and what you owe them. Credit cards, installment loans (like car loans and so forth), and secured creditors like mortgage and home equity lines.

Put the credit cards away. You'll make a stronger case if you aren't piling up more debt at the same time you're asking for forgiveness. So take as many credit cards as possible completely out of circulation. You may need one for ordinary household expenses, but one only.

In writing, please. It's probably best to write a physical letter and mail it to the creditor using the address on the statement. Give it a week or two, then follow it up with a phone call to their customer service line. That will get your situation noted in the online service record as well, and the agents may be able to refer you to an in-house specialist.

Don't be afraid to get help. Organizations like the Consumer Credit Counseling Service can give you tips and help you make contacts. Generally, you should not have to pay for such services.

Tip #31: Make It a Team Effort

Go ahead, crawl into the shell. After all, it's your fault you got laid off, lost your job, had to quit your business; so why would anyone else want to help you? Why should anyone else have to sacrifice to make up for what happened to you?

It's a common way of thinking. But at times like this, recovery is faster if you approach a job loss as a team, a family team, if you have a family. Maybe extended family, maybe your coworkers, friends, and so forth.

Why Is It Important?

As the sayings go, there's no "I" in team, and "*Together Every-one Achieves More.*" You have a cause now—to get a job, restore income, and reduce the financial burn ahead. Get your family members aligned to the task ahead by reducing expenses and being supportive. Ditto for others on the supportive part; you'll be rewarded with a smoother transition—and likely, stronger friend-ships in the end.

What to Do

Family first. It's very important to get your family on board. Tell them what happened—anyone over the age of three should understand eventually. Sit down and work on the family financial plan together, including any adjustments to spending and credit habits necessary. Make a pact, and create a reward system: "When we get this little glitch solved, we're going to take a nice trip or buy that new wakeboard or . . . ." Remember, people who partici-pate in a plan tend to follow it; people who participate in a reward are likely to help achieve it.

Don't be bashful—tell your network. Then, of course, your friends, colleagues, and contacts. Unless you got fired for misconduct, they're likely to be on your side; it can only help. Don't fall for the temptation to keep your problems and "failures" to yourself.

Your spouse is part of the career equation, too. The "macho" male has a tendency to feel responsible—overly responsible—for the family's financial well-being. We males are programmed that way, I guess. And in today's world of working female professionals and stay-at-home dads, it works the other way, too. Don't discount your wife's contributions—they're more important than ever. And if you're the female spouse and have been the primary earner, don't forget about your husband's salary. Check to see where you can make use of your spouse's benefits, like health insurance. For that matter, now may be a good time to put some energy into escalating your spouse's career.

Tip #32: Put It All in Perspective

Getting back on your feet is big, and it's important. But remember, a job ax doesn't chop your head off; it's your chance to move on. With the right combination of attitude and approach, you'll get back on your feet, and perhaps run faster than before. So, here are a few tips that, as you might notice, summarize the previous tips.

Why Is It Important?

Although many feel their career is their life, a job is hardly a life-and-death matter. Sure, money is the means to survival and enjoying many things—but not everything—in life. And career accomplishment and achievement helps you feel better about yourself. Although the length of time unemployed has expanded recently, most are unemployed for six months or less. According to the Bureau of Labor Statistics, the average duration of unemployment was 17.5 weeks in June 2008. Only a third were unemployed for longer than four months, and less than a fifth for longer than six months.

Remember that unemployment is a bump in the road, not the end of the road.

What to Do

Macho isn't best. At the risk of repetition, don't try to hide your situation or burden yourself with 100 percent of the responsibility and blame. As explained next, lots of help is available.

Help is available, so use it. The "macho factor" makes us try to stand tall and take all the hit. We're a little embarrassed, and there's a curious tendency probably ingrained by job experience to try to do everything ourselves to show confidence and self-reliance. Well, those are attractive traits, but you should make use of the help available. Your employer may have resources or may have contracted with some. Check out your state's employment development office as well as the dozens of employment and career counselors, agency websites, and blogs out there. Some give general advice; others take you under their wing and offer services to help you, specifically. Some will charge you for their services, so always make prudent, return-on-investment-oriented decisions.

Keep your brain and body in shape. Nothing makes a worse impression than letting yourself go physically—and mentally, for that matter. Unemployment is a good time not only to keep up your exercise regimen, but to increase it. Not to the point of having a lifeguard tan, mind you, but if you take care of yourself, it will show.

It's a project—manage it like one. You may not be working, but you're still at work—finding your next career step and stage. So manage it like you were managing a work-related enterprise: Keep a schedule; set weekly and monthly goals and routines for your job search, resume building, and networking. The discipline will not only get the job done, it will impress others along the way.

Part II

Hold On to Your Home

Chapter 5

Time for a Crash Diet?

Few things in life can cause more stress or heartache than the prospect of losing your place to live—either as an owner or a renter. It strikes to the core, both emotionally and financially. Disruption, uncertainty, loss, grief, denial, despair—few go through a housing crisis unscathed in some way.

The mortgage crisis that started in 2005 and was egged on by excessively loose lending standards claimed victims on a large scale. People borrowed too much money to buy too much house on the promise that things could only get better. That didn't happen. Market dynamics of supply and demand caught up. New construction increased supply, while a slow economy and low affordability decreased demand. As most Americans borrowed a large percentage of a home's value, thousands—millions—of homeowners were exposed to the same financial truth: Asset values can decline, but the debt used to buy the asset doesn't.

So what does this mean for you, facing an economy that sucks? More uncertainty, for sure. Your income may decline or go away altogether; it's certainly less likely to increase. If your housing cost (rent or mortgage) is already too high as a percentage of your income, you're probably feeling vulnerable; if you're an owner and the house value is dropping, more vulnerable; if you have an adjustable mortgage and the payment is about to increase, still more vulnerable.

The worst thing you can do is go into denial and let things happen to you; you must stay positive and proactive. Take action. There are a lot of solutions out there. Some you can find for yourself, some come in the form of help from others. Above all else, avoid the "f-word"—foreclosure—any way you can.

This chapter and the two that follow will help you manage your personal housing downturn. You'll have to make tough decisions—whether to grit it out, make some adjustments, or sell and move on. Like a job crisis, regardless of the forces at work, regardless of whether it involves everyone or just you, you'll have to deal with it and not panic.

Tip #33: Stop the Bleeding Now

When you're in a hole, stop digging. The clichés are endless but relevant. Even if your home isn't on the line, it's worth taking steps to provide a cushion, a security buffer, to make sure it stays that way. And if it is, the right defensive measures will pay off.

Why Is It Important?

The financial implications can be severe and long lasting. Losing a home is expensive because you'll lose any equity and improvements you have invested in it. There are fees and costs. And foreclosure will disrupt your credit long after the economy gets back on its feet. But there are also the emotional implications—defeat, despair, self-doubt—that can affect you and your relationships for a long time.

It's not a good place to go, and the sooner you can administer first aid, the better. In fact, most advisers suggest confronting a foreclosure as soon as possible, while there's still time to turn back. It's easier, and you'll get more respect from lenders in many cases.

What to Do

Make a plan. Diagnose your situation and sit down, with help where appropriate, to decide what to do. Make an action plan and document it. It will be easier for you to follow and keep family members on board, and it will show good faith to lenders and others (in-laws?) who might help along the way.

Cut up the credit cards. Again, stop digging.

Create a reward. A recurring theme in my experience: People are more likely to sacrifice and act in good faith if there's something in it for them at the end of the road. If you and your family can make the necessary adjustments and endure, why not promise a vacation or a long-desired home improvement when the crisis passes?

Get everyone to agree. You have the plan and the reward; now it's time to get everyone to buy into and sign off on it. Literally, if necessary. All for one, one for all. If everyone isn't on board, you're much more vulnerable.

Tip #34: Measure "The Gap"

It's bad, but how bad? What will it take to reduce or eliminate the financial pain? What will it take to stay in this house? No matter what the financial problem or difficulty, it helps to figure out where you are in real numbers.

Why Is It Important?

As author Katherine Neville put it so well in her novel *The Eight*: "What can be measured can be understood, what can be understood can be altered." Where do you stand with your current expenses? Income? Other resources? The value of your home, if you're an owner? It's important to put it all together before mapping out a defensive plan.

What to Do

Do the numbers. If you haven't done this already, sit down with a sharp pencil (or spreadsheet) and map out all your income from all sources and all your expenses. Clearly identify all your housing expenses—*all* expenses—including mortgage, rent, second mortgages, insurance, taxes, maintenance. Figure your housing costs as a percent of total gross family income. If it's more than 40 percent, that's a bad sign. It's a necessary starting point, and relates to tips in the Financial Forensics chapter.

Analyze your payment(s). If it's a mortgage payment, break it down into interest and any portion that might be going to equity. For that equity portion, it might well make sense to transfer that amount from savings—it's an asset-to-asset transfer. If you have an adjustable or some kind of option mortgage, try to sit down with your lender to clearly map out what might happen. Ditto if it's a rent payment—look at the history and try to estimate, with the landlord's help if you're on good terms, what the future rent might be.

Think about length of time. Don't just focus on how stressed your finances are or what the gap is between what you have and what you need. If your problem is short term, like a job loss or some other income interruption, look at how long that condition might last. The average job separation lasts a little more than four months, so your gap may only have to cover this amount of time.

Tip #35: Appraise the Market

If you're concerned about how affordable your home is or might be in the future, the value of that home is an important consideration. In particular, look at where that value is headed.

Why Is It Important?

Your home is, first, your home; second, it's an investment. So if the value is growing like the good old days of 2003–2006, great. You're getting to live in it, and it's a good investment, too. If the value is steady, you're still getting to live in it, although it may not be such a good investment.

If the value of your home is declining, you've gotta really be in love with it, or it could be real, real expensive. Why? Because you're paying the expenses—mortgage, insurance, upkeep—and you're losing value or equity—a double whammy. So, it's important to see where you are and which way the "puck" is going.

You need to know what you're fighting for.

What to Do

Arm yourself with facts. The "home values" page at Yahoo! Real Estate (*http://realestate.yahoo.com*) is a good place to start, giving an appraisal range and actual recent sales history in your area. This page connects to Zillow (*www.zillow.com*), where you can get a "zestimate" of your home value, and to eppraisal.com, another appraisal site giving typically higher values. The new Home Values page at the National Association of Realtors website (*www.realtor .com*) is another source. Get as many looks as possible, but don't choose the highest one just because you like it.

Understand what's different about your home. The appraisal sites can only do so much with the information they have. Unique features and décor aren't usually counted, and the sites do only a so-so job of building in the quality of your area. If your home is unique or in a unique area, give yourself extra points. If it is ordinary, in an area with excessive building, far from places of work, or just in a so-so neighborhood, be realistic.

Contact a real-estate professional or two. Ask them about the past, present, and future value of your home. Talk to more than one—it's subjective and opinions vary. Also, take advice with a grain of salt. Of course, they'd like you to hear a good number so you'd be tempted to sell. Explain why you need their help.

If still unsure, contact a professional appraiser. If you're still not sure after doing your homework and talking to real-estate professionals, a professional appraisal, though costing a few hundred dollars, might be wise.

Tip #36: Tap All Your Resources

I've already talked about making a list of what you have. Now you need to figure out how to use it to hold on to your home. Once again, take inventory of every little bit you might have stashed away somewhere you can devote to keeping your home going.

Why Is It Important?

Your mortgage or rent payment, if you're like most Americans, is your biggest expense, and if you own your home, it's your biggest investment. So it's worth fighting for. And unless you're in a really bad upside-down condition, it's worth pulling out most, if not all, of the stops.

What to Do

Savings resources. List all savings resources, and find out how liquid they are—that is, how easy it is to access them. Regular savings and checking come first, of course. Stocks and other investments are usually less liquid, but you can sell or borrow against them in a pinch. CDs and other investments are available but with penalties, though typically, the "penalty" of home stress or losing your home is larger.

What to tap first. If you're getting behind on housing costs, your emergency fund (Tip #8) is a good place to start, but try to leave some behind for other emergencies, too. Any investments, including company stock plans, options, and others, are fair game—unless they're far underwater, too. A good plan will probably take a little from this pot, a little from that pot to avoid decimating any single pillar of your financial well-being.

What to avoid. Your retirement investments should be considered a last resort, and may not be a good idea at all. The problem is this: You can't "borrow" your retirement! If you don't have enough funds set aside, too bad! And you're likely to face penalties and taxes on those withdrawals, which can gobble up to 50 percent of the value. Finally, if you're thinking about borrowing from a 401(k) plan, do so only very carefully—those loans are immediately payable upon losing your job—a double whammy!

Use other resources. Just like becoming unemployed, if you're in trouble on your home, now is not the time to crawl into a shell and be afraid to ask. Perhaps family members—your parents or in-laws—could step in to help. They won't give you money for a Jet Ski or a Mini Cooper, but they just might help you avert a crisis.

Tip #37: What Can You Downsize?

You've made the decision that your home is important, worth hanging on to, worth sacrificing for. Your family is in agreement.

Now it's time to put a plan into play to "make room" for your housing cost. Sure, you might reduce that cost through refinancing or some other longer-term change (discussed in the next chapter), but right now the cost is the cost.

Why Is It Important?

Life is full of tradeoffs, and if you're behind the eight ball on housing cost and choose to stay that course, you must sacrifice somewhere else. So, it's time—you and family—to take a very broad, open-minded view of what costs and other obligations you can get rid of. Sure, those cuts might hurt, but not as much as losing your home. That's the choice being made.

What to Do

Evaluate your other debts. Your home is likely your biggest debt, and you have to get rid of some others to service this one. Okay, that's obvious. But now's the time to put your best effort into paying down other debts if you can, and if you can't, making sure they don't get bigger. I've seen it happen—people focus on their house only to lose focus on everything else. You know what happens next.

Look at your long-term goals. Every family has short- and long-term goals—college for the kids, a new pickup truck, a bigger kitchen. If you're having troubles, it's time to trim those goals. In particular, if you have college savings—it's a tough call—such savings can be put into play. Why? There are lots of ways to finance college, and you'll have time to recoup and recover. It would be better than losing your home to foreclosure.

Big-ticket items. There's no time like a housing crisis to look at the big-ticket items you own and decide if you really need them. Expensive cars, car payments, boats, RVs—you get the idea. Not only do these items tie up capital and in many cases add to debt, they also add to expense. A triple whammy. Nobody will look at you funny if you sell that BMW and buy a five-year-old Ford Taurus if it saves your home.

Think about the small stuff. Everybody's got a laundry list of small expenses they could probably do without. From the ever-popular financial target Starbucks latte to the gym membership to the monthly pedicure to beer, wine, and soda in the fridge—it should all be on the table.

The home itself. Not until the other possibilities are considered, but you may need to put this one in play, too. It's a big decision, but maybe you can move in with parents or some other connection for a short time and rent out your home. A lot has to go right to make that work, but it can get you through a crisis. You can also consider selling and moving into a more modest space. See Chapter 9 for more money-saving ideas.

Tip #38: New Income Sources? Be Creative

Sure, it would be nice to have more money. And if your expenses are gobbling you up, it would be especially great. Desperate times call for desperate measures. It won't work for everyone, but if you think a bit outside the box, you may find some additional sources of income that can help you through.

Why Is It Important?

As mentioned earlier, a personal housing crisis most likely will involve some sacrifices and tradeoffs to meet obligations and save your home. You may choose to give up savings, sell assets, or give up some time and or some freedom to make it all happen. And in some cases, producing more income today leads to a better standard of living in the future, should you decide to continue along that path.

What to Do

Add a "family member." No, I'm most certainly not talking about more offspring—that would hardly be the thing to do when times are tight and you're facing downsizing, right? Rent a room or make some other provision to add a boarder. It's something that was once much more common, but can be done today (especially in many of America's outsized homes). It can add a few hundred to a thousand dollars a month in extra income—a big deal. There are lots of possible arrangements, and some of them may already involve family or people you know. Some possible renters may be folks in a similar situation, no longer able to handle their outsized housing costs. Once you and your family make the appropriate adjustments, it can turn out to be a win-win situation.

Get a second job, get a second income. It's common these days—and entirely appropriate—to take some form of a second job or part-time work to get through a tough stretch. Think outside the box. You can work in a retail store. Many these days need staff most when you're probably available, and can accommodate your work hours. You can teach a class for a local community college or grade papers for a testing service or help people learn how to use computers—the possibilities are endless. Talk to temp agencies and let your network know you're looking for something.

It isn't forever. Really, this should be part of the previous two points, but I thought it was important enough to call out separately. An extra roommate or extra job stops far short of being a forever commitment. It's a sacrifice and an effort to get by on your own. It can make you even more proud, at the end of the day, to be a homeowner. And you may gain a job or an experience you can use down the road.

Tip #39: Find a New Place to Borrow

Generally accepted personal-financial principles say don't go into debt unless you have to. Debt should be used for important stuff or where the long-term value is greater than the cost and exposure associated with debt. Arguably, if buying your home had any merit in the first place, borrowing temporarily to keep it in place, to keep it yours, can make sense.

Why Is It Important?

Of course, that's the important decision—should you have bought the home in the first place? By borrowing, would you simply be throwing good money after bad? As the saying goes, when you're in a hole, it's time to stop digging. But if borrowing more will help fill the hole and get you to a better place long term, it's worth pulling out the stops.

The most obvious longer-term solution is refinancing, which comes in the next chapter. Short of that larger effort, here are some borrowing sources to check out.

What to Do

Ask in-laws, family members. Okay, it's hat-in-hand time, but if you have good family relations it doesn't hurt to ask. A family member may have money earning very low interest rates (common during a downturn). You need money and are willing to pay something between tiny savings rates and exorbitant credit card rates—perhaps the current mortgage rate—a possible win-win situation. Make it a formal agreement that helps both parties and helps at tax time, too, else the loan might count as a gift in the eyes of the IRS.

Talk to employers. Believe it or not, many employers recognize that stressed employees are unproductive employees, and they have informal or even formal programs in place to help distressed homeowners. It doesn't hurt to ask.

Other assets—life insurance, securities. You may have other long-forgotten assets as a source of temporary funds. Check out options to borrow against insurance policies or brokerage accounts. You must be careful with the latter—declining stock prices can cause these loans to be called, if through a broker (known as a margin call), at the worst possible time, so talk to an adviser or professional before making this move.

Consider 401(k), credit cards—but be careful. Borrowing on 401(k) plans or credit cards are akin to playing with fire. As mentioned above, 401(k) loans are callable upon termination, so if you get laid off, blam! And credit-card interest is a very expensive way to hang on to anything—you'll dig another hole to get out of the original one.

Don't borrow your way out of debt. During better times, loan marketers talked of bill consolidation and borrowing on home equity to reduce interest rates. It generally isn't a good idea, especially if you're borrowing long term to fix a short-term problem. The immediate problem might go away, but you'll deal with the consequences for years. If your problem is short term, borrow short term, if at all.

Tip #40: Don't Do This Alone

Help is what other people are for, especially those trained and experienced in financial matters. You wouldn't tackle a legal problem without legal help, so why would you try it with a financial one?

Why Is It Important?

Second opinions from unbiased and uninvolved individuals who have seen similar problems before can be really helpful. Of course, you must be sure these folks are truly unbiased and not trying to sell you something.

What to Do

Talk to a smart friend. When my computer breaks, my first call goes to an "expert" friend. Not only is the help free and unencumbered of any other motives, but my friend understands me and how I use my computers. So if you have a best friend, it's time to get some friendly advice. If that friend is good with financial stuff, so much the better.

Consult a financial professional. Professional financial advisers are trained to run the numbers and consider all aspects of your situation and the big picture. Compensation is the hard part—they make money from sales commissions, by charging hourly fees, or some combination of the two. A fee-based or fee-only Certified Financial Planner (CFP®) is best, but your bank officer, stockbroker, insurance agent, or others can also give you a hand.

Go into credit counseling. When times are tough, credit counseling agencies are busy places. Trained and experienced pros can give advice and help you restructure your debt. Again, make sure it's a nonprofit organization with strong credentials and without a sales pitch. A dot.org website and membership in National Foundation for Credit Counseling (*www.nfcc.org*) and the Association of Independent Consumer Credit Counseling Agencies (*www.aiccca.org*) are good indications it's legit.

Mortgage counseling. Credit counselors can help you with general debt issues, including housing debt. But if foreclosure is a real possibility or the structure of the mortgage itself is the issue, specialized mortgage counselors are available to help you through the options and initiate conversations with lenders, something that can be hard to do on your own. Hope Now (*www.hopenow.com*) is the largest and most important agency. It is a government and industry sponsored consortium set up to help you through the maze, and there are others as well. More in the next chapter.

Chapter 6

Renegotiate, Refinance, but Don't Renege

The July 2008 headline "More Foreclosure Gloom" rang loud and clear across the country. And boy, was there ever more foreclosure gloom. Some 220,000 homes were lost to banks just in the second quarter of that year, triple the number in 2007.

Ouch. And foreclosure realty specialist RealtyTrac had been forecasting 1.9 to 2 million foreclosures for all of 2008. That number reached 1.4 million by June, forcing the agency to reach for a new forecast.

And while real-estate markets are considered "local," the fore-closure phenomenon was hardly so, with forty-eight of fifty states and ninety-five of 100 metro areas experiencing increases in foreclosures.

When times are good, a few unlucky or unwise folks get trapped in homes too big or expensive for them to afford. Or some other unforeseen calamity strikes—a job loss, health situation, business failure. When times are tough, income stress is greater, and foreclosures typically go up, but not like they did in 2007–2008. Home values dropped and payments for many homeowners locked into so-called ARMs (Adjustable Rate Mortgages) went up. A perfect storm followed. A perfect storm of ordinary, unsuspecting folks finding themselves under water with debts exceeding home values. From a real-estate point of view, the economy sucked as never before.

So what is a foreclosure? How does it affect personal finances? Why is it so important to avoid a foreclosure filing and what can you do about it? How do you defend yourself against foreclosure, or nip it in the bud before it gets started? What should you do if it does get started? What are the options, and how should you handle yourself and your finances during the crisis?

Tip #41: Know the High Cost of Foreclosure

So what if you can't make it anymore? Why not just turn in the keys and walk away? Or let them go through their process and "stick it to them" by hanging on as long as possible?

Because a full foreclosure, where a lender repossesses your home, is one of the worst things that can happen to you financially—and emotionally.

Why Is It Important?

It's a big deal: You lose any value you had in the home, including down payments, paid-in equity, and improvements; your credit rating takes a big hit—you might not be able to borrow for a home or for anything else for years; your confidence and reputation take a big hit, too. Potential creditors avoid you, for sure, but a foreclosure can also hurt you in the eyes of future employers, insurance companies, even cell phone providers. Unfortunately, in the eyes of a great many others, it becomes a matter of trust.

What to Do

A ten-year hiatus. A full foreclosure, where the lender takes possession and is forced to resell the property, may create a blemish on your credit record for seven to ten years—longer than most other bad things. The good news: While a foreclosure is bad, it isn't as bad as a bankruptcy. There's some evidence that with the glut of foreclosures in 2007–2008 and the role of lenders in getting people into unaffordable loans, foreclosures won't ding your credit score as much as in the past. But it's a big ding, nevertheless. Not only will credit be harder to come by, you'll pay higher interest rates and encounter tougher credit terms.

Income taxes. If you borrow and receive money for someone, and that debt is eventually forgiven or discharged by some other means than paying it back, the amount not paid back is considered to benefit you financially, so it's taxable income. So many folks who couldn't pay a mortgage balance, even with the proceeds of selling a home, were hit with a nasty tax surprise—a tax bill on tens, even hundreds of thousands of dollars of relieved debt. The good news is that Federal income tax was largely done away with through 2013 by the Emergency Economic Stabilization Act of 2008, if the home involved is your primary residence and certain other conditions apply. The bad news is that this law only covers Federal taxes, and you may still face state income-tax liability.

Continued pursuit. In many states, if your home is taken away in foreclosure and you still owe money to a lender after your home is sold and proceeds are applied to your loan, creditors can still come after you for the remainder due. You may still owe on the loan—with additional interest—and may not be notified for months or even years. There are thirty-eight states in which such *deficiency judgments* are possible and practical.

Tip #42: Know the Players

To successfully navigate your way through your housing crisis, you must know who the players are and what they want.

Why Is It Important?

At the end of the day, you're looking for a win-win solution. You want to get out of your crisis with your home, and if possible, your credit, intact, but others have a stake in the game, too. Investors—the folks at the end of the food chain who provided the money you borrowed—want their money back. The lender—who put you together with the investor or may be the investor itself—doesn't want your real estate; in a downturn, they probably have enough already. And the servicer makes money servicing your loan, so it wants to keep your business. Despite the stories you may have heard, everybody involved is looking to minimize losses. Keep this in mind as you move forward.

What to Do

Know the lender. The lender is the bank or mortgage company who granted you the loan. They are also the party that will end up with your property if it is foreclosed. They may or may not have sold your loan to an investor. If you borrowed from a local bank, a credit union, or a large national mortgage banker with a banking subsidiary, like Countrywide, chances are higher that they kept the loan. As a result, they may have more latitude to negotiate with you.

Know the servicer. Most lenders turn the loan over to a servicer, who mails statements, collects your payments, and updates your balance. The servicer is usually the first to notify you and the lender of a problem. The servicer is your first point of contact to get it resolved. Many forget this and go to the lender. The lender isn't staffed to deal with your situation; the servicer is supposed to be. Many lenders won't deal with you directly until the foreclosure process is formally begun—which may be too late for a clean workout. So don't go to the lender first unless it's a credit union or someone local you've dealt with for years.

Know the investor–if possible. Investors provided the money you borrowed typically by investing in securities packaged and sold by the lender. About half of all mortgage funds are provided by government-backed Fannie Mae and Freddie Mac. Funds are also provided by large institutional funds, like pension funds, bond funds, money-market funds, or even foreign governments either directly or through investments in Fannie or Freddie securities. They care about one thing—getting their money back.

Know the credit bureau. There are three credit bureaus—Experian, Equifax, and TransUnion. All three track your credit history, including payments, outstanding balances, credit limits, and overall credit habits. If you have a delinquency, they'll find out from your servicer; if you have a foreclosure, they'll find out from your lender. These events become part of your history and your mathematical *credit score*, which each agency calculates.

Know the mortgage counselor. This is a new group of government- or community-sponsored agencies set up to help you navigate your way through a housing crisis and contact the right people with the right workout proposal.

Tip #43: Know the Foreclosure "Script"

You thought buying your home was complicated and scary and full of terminology and paperwork you could barely be expected to understand? Try going through a foreclosure. It varies state by state, involves more legal wrangling, and there are no equivalents to real-estate agents lined up to explain it to you.

Why Is It Important?

Like most financial things, it helps to understand how it all works so you know what's going on, how to react and respond, and where to get help. Delinquency and foreclosure are bad enough without surprises. If you can get your problem resolved either through a workout or by selling it before the Notice Of Default (NOD) goes out, you'll save a lot of trouble. However, you may have trouble getting anyone's attention to do a workout before the NOD—and then it might be too late.

Following is a rough outline of the process, which will vary some by state. The best place to find more detail on state-by-state specifics is to contact state HUD offices, foreclosure real-estate specialist Realtytrac (*http://www.realtytrac.com/foreclosure/overview.html*), or engage with a mortgage counselor.

What to Do

Grace period (0–30 days). Most lenders have a thirty-day grace period for late payments, so if you're just a little late, you don't have much to worry about. If you're stressed, it's a good idea to check your grace period and the fees associated with it. If there is no grace period, foreclosure proceedings can begin almost immediately.

Late payment (30–60 days). If you're more than thirty days late, the alarm bells start to go off. You might get a phone call or letter from your servicer. Depending on your loan agreement, you may have to settle both months—the current month and the overdue month—to get current.

Notice of default (60–90 days). At this point (and the timeline varies both by state and by loan contract), it becomes official. Your case becomes a legal one and your lender can initiate action to repossess your home and or sell it to others. Depending on the jurisdiction, you still have time—thirty days or so—to work something out.

Notice of sale (90–120 days). A court determines that a lender can start sale proceedings, sometimes through auction. In a "power of sale" state, a deed of trust is drawn up temporarily conveying the property to a trustee who will sell the house, also sometimes through auction. At this point, you'll be evicted from the home if you haven't been already, and it's generally too late to work anything out.

Auction or REO. Once the foreclosure process is completed, the property is either sold or retained by the bank (lender) as "Real Estate Owned." It's theirs and theirs to sell. Typically, they sell it themselves or hire special agencies to sell it, but by that time the game's over for you.

Tip #44: Find Out Your Options

Chapter 5 dealt with ways to see the crisis coming and avert it by adjusting income and expenses to make ends meet. But suppose it isn't possible—now what? What can you do to get out from under your mortgage? How can you find the win-win that either keeps you in your home or gets you out of it in a financially face-saving way? There are generally three possibilities: a workout, which temporarily or permanently adjusts loan terms; refinancing, which replaces the loan, usually with better terms; or a sale, which (hopefully) pays off the loan and allows you to move on.

Why Is It Important?

Knowing the options helps you know what questions to ask, what kind of help to seek from the players involved, and what a mortgage counselor might be doing for you.

What to Do

Consider a workout. There are many ways to adjust loan terms to help you in the short term. A so-called *forbearance* allows you to pay something less than the full payment for a specified period.

The lender doesn't give anything away—the amount not paid will usually be added to the loan balance. It may be accompanied by a documented repayment plan. Some workouts might go further to extend the terms of the loan (thus lowering payments). In a few cases, lenders are agreeing to lower loan balances or foregoing interest-rate adjustments on ARMs, but this is uncommon, as it's difficult to get the investors to agree to these terms. A solid understanding of the process, good relations with your lender and servicer, a good understanding of your finances, and an effective mortgage counselor will all help.

Consider refinance. If your current loan is untenable, it may be possible to get a new one. Of course, the hardest time to get a loan is when you need one. The process will be further complicated if your home value has fallen or if you have a second loan or line of credit on the home. But if your credit is still good and you're in an ARM or bit off a little too much with a fifteen-year mortgage, refinancing might work. At the time of this writing, new Federal laws are working to make refinancing easier, but still not a walk in the park. See Tip #45.

Find a buyer now. If you're in trouble and can save a bigger fall (like losing your home) by selling now, even at a reduced price, it makes sense. See Chapter 7.

Consider a deed in lieu of foreclosure. This complicated-sounding term could be called "voluntary surrender." You work out a deal with the bank to give them the deed in exchange for no further liability and a clean(er) credit record. Of course, you lose the value of your down payment and any improvements, but your credit stays clean. The process is simple, but banks overloaded with REO may not be interested, and it gets more complicated if there are other liens, like a second mortgage or equity line, on the property.

Arrange a short sale. A short sale is done before a notice of sale and is an agreement with the lender to let you sell the property for less than the full amount due. You then give the proceeds to the lender. Again, you come out with nothing from the sale, but you avoid a foreclosure on your credit record. In the 2007–2008 real estate decline, short sales became popular mostly because of excessive REO inventory at banks. In normal times, short sales are uncommon.

Tip #45: Know Where the Government Can Help

Most people who own homes are, at least to some degree, programmed to solve their own problems—it's part of the nature of home ownership. However, when the economy sucks, economic forces can overwhelm even the most self-reliant individuals. The mortgage crisis of 2007–2008 was big enough to merit more government assistance than we've seen in years, since the Great Depression, really. Government programs offer advice and tactical assistance and can help you refinance into a more favorable loan with an assortment of tax breaks along the way. They are complicated, overlapping in some cases, and rapidly evolving. Getting engaged will take some research and patience.

Why Is It Important?

While it's rewarding (and usually simpler) to work out your own problems, it makes sense to check out government programs, which apply to a growing circle of eligible citizens.

What to Do

Take advantage of counseling services. Federal, state, and in some cases, local governments have set up an assortment of counseling services to help you navigate through a crisis and get the help you need. The largest is Hope Now (*www.hopenow.com*).

Look into military exemptions. If you're having problems because of military service, the Servicemembers Civil Relief Act calls for more favorable terms and can prevent foreclosure—but you must contact your lender to do a workout.

FHA Secure. Announced in August 2007, this was the first refinancing initiative announced by the Federal government. The idea
is to help people refinance mortgages, especially ARMs, into fixed
FHA-backed loans not requiring mortgage insurance. Targeted to
homeowners who are still current, FHA has also asked lenders to
approve loans for customers with minor delinquencies. See
www.fha.gov and go to the "FHA Secure" link.

Check out Project Lifeline. An informal February 2008 deal
between the Federal government (U.S. Treasury and HUD) and
six major mortgage lenders covering about 50 percent of the mortgage market, it extends the foreclosure timeline for those on the
brink (more than ninety days past due). Lawmakers also raised the
limit on so-called conforming mortgages, making it easier to
refinance.

Read the 2008 "Housing Rescue Bill." In 2008, the Federal government passed the largest mortgage and housing relief bill in
U.S. history. For key provisions, see sidebar below.

Find out about home repair and vacant home programs. Com-
munities have recognized the impact and burden of vacant homes
on home values and general community well-being, and a patch-
work of loan and assistance programs have emerged. On a national
scale, the National Community Reinvestment Coalition champi-
ons the cause (*www.ncrc.org*), and if you dig deep, especially in a
hard-hit area, you may find state or local help. The 2008 housing
rescue bill also directs funds to this cause.

Tax relief. The Federal government has stepped in with the
Mortgage Forgiveness Debt Relief Act of 2007 to avoid socking
people with tax bills on forgiven loans. The 2008 housing rescue
bill adds a $7,500 tax credit for first-time buyers directed at stim-
ulating purchase of homes in distress or foreclosure—although
that credit must be returned to the government over time.

Learn about state programs. The Federal government is not the
only source of help—most state governments have stepped in with
programs of their own. The best way to find them is to search
something like "mortgage assistance Ohio" or find the state Hous-

ing and Urban Development or similar department website. Some counseling programs are state run and most will point you to state resources.

A $300 BILLION RESCUE

In July 2008, the president and Congress passed a large and wide-ranging housing bill designed mainly to come to the relief of as many as 2 million homeowners. Called the American Housing Rescue and Foreclosure Prevention Act of 2008, the bill provides an aggressive FHA-backed refinancing plan. Qualifying homeowners receiving loans between January 2005 and January 2007 who spend at least 31 percent of their gross income on a mortgage, in default or not, and who can prove that they can't keep up with their existing mortgage, can get a favorable fixed-rate, FHA-backed mortgage. They can't take out any other form of equity loan on the home for five years, and there are provisions to prevent investors from taking advantage and to recapture some of the appreciation you as a homeowner may realize in future years. Details can be found by entering the name of the law into a search engine.

Tip #46: Initiate Contact Now

The various resources and counseling services out there all agree on one thing: If you're in trouble, or even think you might be in trouble, get started as soon as possible. Initiate contact with your servicer, your lender, or with a counseling agency.

Why Is It Important?

People have a curious tendency to look the other way when it comes to bad news, especially bad financial news. They focus on life's other aspects and hope the problem will go away.

Unfortunately, this is the exact wrong path, and the more you get behind and the farther the foreclosure process goes, the harder your crisis is to fix.

What to Do

Open your mail. Don't just file those letters from your lender or servicer in the stack. Keep close tabs on your savings and other resources, too, to avoid nasty surprises. Yes, it's hard.

Start the process. While lenders, servicers, and counselors are busy folks these days, it pays to take the initiative. You may not succeed—there are still stories of lenders refusing to talk to borrowers until they're ninety days late—when a notice of default has already going out. But the fact you tried will help you look proactive in a lender's eyes, and you may just get someone ready and willing to help. Pick up the phone and write letters. Remember, lenders don't want foreclosure, either.

Servicer first. Most advisers still recommend contacting the loan servicer—the folks who send your statements and take your payments—first. They'll note that you called and may tell you whom to talk to in order to start a workout. If you get stonewalled, a counseling service is probably next—they'll help you get connected to the right people. If your lender is local—a local bank or credit union or a friendly branch of a larger bank—that can be a good place to start.

Be persistent. It's your financial life—don't give up. Yes, it will be difficult, and yes, you'll run into some walls. Persistence, cool tempers, and a methodical approach get the best results.

Tip #47: Figure Out What You Can Afford to Pay

In the spirit of what can be understood can be altered, it pays to know, before you start talking workout or refinance, what you can really afford to pay. Be honest, but also be creative.

Why Is It Important?

Lenders and everyone else up and down the line appreciate borrowers who are in trouble but knowledgeable and realistic about their situation; they're easier to work with. Be honest with yourself and the parties you engage—if not, you'll end up in the same predicament, or worse.

What to Do

Take a complete picture of your finances. Regular and irregular income, regular and irregular expenses. Write it down. You've probably done some of this. Chapter 8, "Financial Forensics," and other tips in this book can help.

Scenarios, please. A good go-forward financial plan has a few what-ifs. Do a few scenario plans reflecting income or expense "bad news" and "good news." It's part of preparation, and lenders may appreciate the realistic risk assessment.

Contact other creditors. Mortgage lenders aren't the only ones facing the credit crunch, and they aren't the only ones who might be willing to help you survive. It pays to contact credit card issuers and other creditors to see if you can stretch your payments a bit— which might help you find a few dollars more for your mortgage payment. Beware of fees or other unfavorable terms.

Tip #48: Help Is Nearby: Go to a Mortgage Counselor

In the spirit of not going it alone, and with the frenetic pace and overwhelming workload of most of the players in the mortgage industry during a downturn (especially a housing induced downturn like 2007–2008), a qualified intermediary can help.

Why Is It Important?

Counseling agencies can help you figure out where you are, structure your inquiry and proposal, and get you connected to the

right people. In doing that, they can help you get to a solution
with as little frustration as possible. With the amount of experience gained in the 2007–2008 housing crisis, these agencies have
become more effective and have gained credibility.

What to Do

Check out national agencies. Hope Now is the best example.
Founded with support from HUD and the Treasury Department,
Hope Now is a complex alliance of debt counselors, servicers, and
other mortgage-industry players. Their mission is to "standardize
and facilitate the process for mortgage holders to engage the right
parties to solve problems," and to help people when thirty to sixty
days late "before they go over the edge." The website is *www
.hopenow.com*, and the hotline is 1-888-995-HOPE. It's the largest and most effective agency in play today.

Check out state agencies. Most states also offer hotlines to answer
foreclosure questions and connect homeowners to the right people. Typically sponsored by a consortium of public and private
interests, they're designed to educate homeowners on what's coming and what to do about it—and to be as proactive as possible.
The Colorado Foreclosure Hotline is a good example, and you can
use the HUD "Local HUD Information" page to find affiliated
agencies (*http://www.hud.gov/local/index.cfm*).

Try other agencies. Several agencies targeted to the needs of specific socioeconomic groups like the elderly, not surprisingly, recognize the seriousness of housing issues and are aligned to offer
help. Many can be found at the Federal HUD site "National and
Regional Counseling Intermediaries" page: *http://www.hud.gov/
offices/hsg/sfh/hcc/nrhci.cfm*.

Tip #49: Get a Legal Review

If you're legitimately behind on payments, it probably makes more sense to solve that problem and move on than to fight tooth and nail with lenders over every inch of the procedure. Good relations lead to win-win solutions. However, there are some standard legal protections that could help, and there have been many documented cases of lenders stepping over the line out of aggressiveness or sometimes plain ignorance of the terms of your loan. Remember—an awful lot of mortgages were generated in the past few years, some by people new to the business, all in a hurry.

Why Is It Important?

Mostly, you want to check what you actually signed up for. There are laws to protect you, like the 1968 Truth in Lending Act, which specifies disclosure requirements, and the Servicemembers Civil Relief Act, which protects military personnel. Not only is it worth double checking a lender's right to foreclose, but there can be a lot of fees involved, and there have been abuses there, too.

What to Do

Start with a mortgage counselor. A good counselor (see Tip #48) should be able to point out the right legal checks. But if you're not sure everything's being covered, a one-hour consultation with an attorney might be a good ticket.

Determine the right to foreclose. Lenders can initiate foreclosure if principal and interest, property tax, or insurance payments have been missed. But sometimes there's a mix-up, or there's some other clause in the loan protecting the borrower. Also, make sure the party initiating foreclosure actually has the right to do so—typically the servicer, sometimes the lender, never the investor or any other agency.

Watch for common errors. Terms of the loan must be right, as must be the computation of interest and any fees. If you've already received a workout or forbearance, make sure the terms of that agreement are honored. Mortgage servicers are very busy—make sure they've credited all your payments and that their records agree with yours. If necessary, get help from an expert with a financial calculator to make sure principal and interest have been properly calculated and credited, or ask the servicer for a review.

Look at the disclosure requirements. The Truth in Lending Act is pretty specific, and special provisions cover ARM loans, what they based interest-rate calculations on, and the notifications that must occur as terms change. It's worth checking disclosures, especially if you have an ARM.

Avoid junk charges. Look at your mortgage statements and default notices carefully. Make sure to avoid or question unreasonable "service" or "late" or "referral" fees. There should be no charges not specifically called out in your loan docs.

Consider rescission. If there's a violation of Truth in Lending requirements, and you've been in the loan for less than three years, it may be possible to effectively cancel the loan and start over. It may also be possible to get a lender to modify terms. But this is a last-ditch tactic not to be relied upon unless you have a strong case.

Tip #50: Keep Excellent Records

If you're in a crisis and about to start the tricky process of working your way out of it, be organized, and don't forget to keep excellent records of everything you say, everything they say, when it was said, and so forth.

Why Is It Important?

First, it's complicated. You already knew that. But it's also very delicate. And everyone's in a hurry, bombarded from left to right by other borrowers and investors. There's a lot of pressure. And in times of pressure, mistakes are made and things that are said become forgotten. You'll also be able to respond or provide information more quickly and clearly.

What to Do

Find the best written communication channel. Some organizations function better with e-mail, some with paper. Find out which will work best—just ask.

Write letters. Don't just say it, don't just make phone calls, back everything up in writing. "I'm writing this letter to summarize the conversation and agreement we came to on such-and-forth day for future reference." Then the content. Then "If there are any questions or corrections, please advise."

Keep a journal. Compiling a master journal noting all communications—date, time, and with whom you spoke—comes in handy as a master record of what happened, and as a place to keep any additional details. Sounds like project management doesn't it?—and yes, it is. Solving a real estate crisis is a project.

Keep copies of all correspondence. It's a good idea to set up a binder with all letters, documents, and printed e-mails. Again, the singular reference source for anything you might need to move forward or back something up is essential, else you'll waste time, and valuable info can be lost.

Tip #51: Avoid Scams

When times get tough, the scammers get organized. It's inevitable, and it's happened since the beginning of time. These unscrupulous operators figure we're all driven by emotion and incapable of making a rational decision when our backs are to the wall, especially when time is of the essence, as it is in a mortgage situation. Not you! You bought this book and are reading it to be informed and make rational decisions.

Why Is It Important?

Of course you want to avoid scams, which will cost money, put you into a deeper hole—or worse. Mortgages and foreclosures are relatively unfamiliar territory for most folks. The trick is to see a scam coming, or if you aren't sure, just put it on ignore.

What to Do

Know the major scams. Most involve someone coming in and buying you out of your home. Some offer to lease it back to you, others will promise to work out a refinance while the clock ticks. These things don't happen, don't happen on a timely basis, or the terms change when your back gets to the wall. Your home may be foreclosed anyway, and in some cases, the "rescuer" could end up keeping your equity if there is any. Look out.

Avoid them if they use fancy words like "loss mitigation" or call themselves "certified consultants." There are no such professions, and while the terminology of mortgage and foreclosure is unfamiliar and confusing, what you're really looking for is "help" or a "work-out" or a "refi"—simple stuff like that.

If they come to you, watch out. The only person who should be coming to you is the servicer (or lender, if they do their own servicing). And if their pitch is "Let us help," lock your shields in a full defensive position.

If it seems too good to be true. . . . The phrase holds here as everywhere.

Chapter 7

Moving On When You Must

As they say about relationships, sometimes it just isn't meant to be. You may have bought your house with great expectations during the greatest of times: good career; robust income; opportunity to grow income; strong economy; healthy income for your spouse, too; and an energetic real-estate market—if not in boom, at least healthy enough to expect single-digit price increases each year. But it didn't turn out that way. The economy faltered. Something in your personal economy faltered, like a health crisis or disability. And the housing market faltered. Or, as happened to many in 2007–2008, all three at once, the perfect storm.

Whatever the circumstance, it isn't going to work. You've come to realize that maybe the house just isn't going to fit into your long-term plans.

There is good news, however. First, if you made that decision, it's probably a rational one, and you're well on your way to making more rational choices about its disposal.

Second, while for most people it's their biggest investment, it isn't their life. It's just a home. Life goes on. There will be other opportunities. The economy will get better. There will be another home. And you'll have learned a lot from the experience.

Third, you're not the only one. In the 2007–2008 downturn, millions went delinquent or into some stage of foreclosure, and hundreds of thousands lost their homes. Millions more had to sell a home they didn't want to sell. It happens, and it happened to a lot of folks. It will set you back financially, and it's emotionally tough, but people understand. Your family and friends still like you. They'll help you. Again, it's a home, not your life.

You'll find that if you're in this situation, there are lots of choices—whether or not to sell, how to sell, where to move, how to adjust your lifestyle to fit your new home. This chapter deals with the voluntary sale or transfer of your home and how to move on from the crisis. The first two tips cover ways to transfer your property to a lender in preforeclosure, that is, to avoid foreclosure. The remainder deals more generally with how to get a home sale done with minimal financial and emotional loss.

Tip #52: Use a Deed in Lieu

If you find yourself unable to keep up with your mortgage, and the loan amount about matches what the home is worth, you might consider just handing the keys to the bank. The transaction is called a deed in lieu of foreclosure.

You want to avoid the pain of foreclosure and the ding to your credit; the lender wants to avoid the cost of the foreclosure. So you transfer the property to the lender, and the lender absolves you of responsibility for the debt. You'll have to connect with the bank and ask; there's no legal requirement that a bank accept or agree to a deed in lieu. Whether it works depends on the situation and whether your lender is eager to avoid the foreclosure process. It is also more difficult if there are other loans or liens on the property.

Why Is It Important?

Effectively, it's a win-win if the amounts match and the lender is prepared to take on the real estate as REO (Real Estate Owned) and dispose of it. The lender saves foreclosure expenses and can get a jump on marketing the property. You get rid of your burden and avoid most of the hit to your credit.

What to Do

Decide if a deed in lieu makes sense. If you're "upside down"—the loan is greater than the property value—the lender will take a hit (and may agree to a short sale—see next tip). If the loan is less than the property value, then you'd lose your equity (though some lenders have been known to settle for the excess amount, but that's rare). A mortgage counselor can help.

List your home with a realtor. Most lenders won't consider a deed in lieu unless you've tried to sell your home on your own.

Engage with lender. Ask about a deed in lieu; be nice, courteous; know your situation well; and be prepared to document it.

Understand fees and tax consequences. You may still be liable for transfer fees and taxes, and if the lender accepts a home worth less than the loan (which happens occasionally), you may have an income-tax liability at least at the state level. (The 2007 Mortgage Forgiveness Debt Relief Act takes care of this problem, for now, at the Federal level.)

Tip #53: Think about a Short Sale

In the stock market, "selling short" means borrowing shares and selling them into the market, hoping to buy them back later at a lower price, thus making a profit. Selling short has a completely different meaning in the real estate world, and it's one that mostly sat in a dark corner until the 2007–2008 real estate bust. A short sale happens when a lender permits a borrower to sell a home, usually to a third party, for less than the value of the mortgage. There's an agreement that the proceeds, even though short of the loan value, will be applied to the debt. The borrower is then discharged from any further obligation.

What's happening is simple. The lender (and investor) is accepting something less than the face value of the loan, but the bank doesn't have to take on the property and dispose of it as an REO. That's important, because banks are busy, have too much REO, and recognize, according to a recent Freddie Mac survey, that the average foreclosure costs them about $58,000 to administer and may take as long as eighteen months. So effectively, the bank is making a concession in order to avoid more real estate on its books and a bigger loss from the foreclosure.

Why Is It Important?

Short sales can work if your loan value modestly exceeds the property value and the bank is overloaded with property. It's good for you because it gets rid of the obligation and avoids the foreclosure ding to your credit report.

What to Do

Try to sell it. A lender is more likely to listen if you've truly tried to sell a home the regular way for a higher value and failed. List it for at least thirty days before making your case.

Detail and document your finances. Lenders won't accept a ding to the loan value if you're indeed able to pay. You must fully analyze your situation and be prepared to show documents to the lender.

Make your case. The lender is under no obligation to do a short sale; you must make your case carefully, diplomatically, and in a businesslike manner. A mortgage counselor can help you make the connections and build the case.

Find a realtor specializing in short sales. Some agents specialize in making fast, below-market sales. Your bank or lender may help you find one.

Keep property in good shape. If you've let the place go to pot, the lender isn't going to want to take the hit for that.

Pay off other liens. A short sale is harder if other parties have to settle, too. Pay them off or make a deal.

Understand tax consequences. You're getting a certain amount of debt forgiveness, which may trigger some income tax, at a state level anyway.

Tip #54: Live Small: The Art of Downsizing

There's an inherent message in any economic downturn: The economy is shrinking. As a whole, we're producing fewer goods and services. And, as seen in the 2007–2008 downturn, for reasons of scarcity and other reasons mostly beyond anyone's control, prices of key staples may actually rise. The economic pie is smaller, there's less to go around, and even if our share is relatively unchanged, the message is clear: We must shrink our standard of living, if only a bit.

So, the natural and sensible response is to adjust—downsize— our standard of living. Spend less. That doesn't mean you'll enjoy life less, just that you'll spend less. You'll learn to be satisfied or happy with a little less economic worth. I talk about this more in the final chapter, "Downsize with Dignity."

Since your home is likely the biggest chunk of your economic life, it may well be where the downsizing starts.

Why Is It Important?

Starting with the home is especially important if you feel that the economic effects will be long term or if you simply want to play defense against becoming overextended again. I'm not talking about going homeless or living in substandard or low-income housing. It's about ideas to keep a reasonably steady lifestyle while spending less on your home.

What to Do

Decide how much home you really need. According to statistics shared by personal finance author David Bach in *Go Green, Live Rich*, the average new home in 1973 was under 1,200 square feet. Between 1978 and 2006, it grew from 1,750 to nearly 2,500 square feet, and today nearly 23 percent of new homes exceed 3,000 square feet. Are people getting bigger? No. Are families getting larger? No again. It's the extra den, the oversized baths, the tennis-court sized master suite, the extra bedrooms. Not only are these homes more expensive to buy, they are more expensive to heat, cool, furnish, and maintain.

Location, location, location. It's a funny thing about American life, that an address is so important. We all want to live in desirable areas or areas with top-notch schools, but don't stop to think about how much this cherry-on-top attribution costs. Choosing a not-quite-perfect neighborhood or even a city can be much, much cheaper, especially if you go for a smaller home at the same time. Rewarding, too—you're doing more with less, and the area has a chance to improve if like-minded people follow your lead.

Consider a different kind of house. You may be accustomed to a certain type of home—a spacious suburban home on a cul-de-sac. But especially in the aftermath of the 2007–2008 downturn, there's a growing trend toward "not-so-big" homes, and many architects and developers are catering to this need. (Grab a copy of architect Sarah Susanka's *The Not So Big House: A Blueprint for the Way We Really Live* to see what I mean and get ideas.) Look at older homes too, which naturally inspired Susanka. Consider the rise of quality and attractively styled manufactured homes from Palm Harbor and other makers, also.

LEARNING MORE ABOUT YOUR NEXT PLACE

Evaluating a new place to live—a new neighborhood, a new city—used to be more an art than a science—if you had any choice at all. You talked to people who lived there—often real-estate agents primed to sell you on the place. Your employer was, of course, sold on the place. You may have driven around to see if it was attractive; to see if residents looked, acted, sounded like you. Nowadays, it's easier to add some "science" to that critical decision. I developed a book with location data specialist Bert Sperling, called *Cities Ranked & Rated—More Than 400 Metropolitan Areas Evaluated in the U.S. and Canada 2ed.* (Wiley, 2007). With it, you can judge jobs, income, cost of living, education, and myriad factors capturing quality of life. Internet resources include (Bert) Sperling's Best Places (*www.bestplaces.net*) and two popular real-estate sites, Zillow (*www.zillow.com*) and Trulia (*www.trulia.com*, "stats and trends" page). All three offer valuable demographic, economic, and school data; the latter two give helpful real-estate price analysis also. Know before you go.

Tip #55: Just Sell It—Getting Ready

If you expect your housing crisis to endure for a while, or if you're just tired of being exposed—overexposed—to the cost of your home, it makes sense to sell. Of course, it's not only a financial but also an emotional decision, one not to be taken lightly and one to be made as a family team.

Why Is It Important?

Once you make the decision, commit to the project. You must prepare, follow, communicate, stay with it to get it done. In a down market, there are more sellers than buyers, and buyers can be choosy and take as much time as they want. So if you're not making a well-planned and well-coordinated effort, various sales inhibitors will get in your way. You won't succeed, and your problems may worsen.

What to Do

Figure out where to go next. Selling your home must be part of a grander plan to relocate yourself and your family. So figure out where you want to go—another home purchase, a rental, an apartment, your in-laws' basement. It's important to know your financial needs in advance, and be prepared to move when you need to. Flexibility is important.

Get the help you need. There's no law saying you must hire specialists (other than an attorney in some states) to sell a home. That's your decision, and in the spirit of saving money and getting to market in your own special way, you may want to sell it yourself (see Tip #57 on FSBO). But the important thing right now is to get it done, and the help of a real-estate professional may just make that happen faster and better in a tight market. Choose carefully; find an agent who does more than just plant a for-sale sign in your front yard; one you feel can, and will, really help you market and sell your home.

Get the price right. Put simply, it isn't 2005–2006 anymore. Easy financing and a boom mentality inflated many real-estate prices beyond recognition. The good news is that while they've retreated, they've retreated to approximately 2004 levels, so if you bought then or before, you're still doing okay. Price accordingly. Too high a price will kill a sale, and sequential price reductions send a signal to the market that you know you were overpriced.

Clean up, fix up, beautify. Like almost anything else you sell, a home is a product, and a buyer is looking to buy quality. While you may have gotten used to a home's "warts"—broken screens, peeling paint, a garage door that doesn't work—a buyer, especially in a buyer's market, will turn the other way. Get your home right before going to market.

Tip #56: Just Sell It—Market Your Home

You've decided to sell. You've set a price, decided on an agent (or not), and gotten the practical details in place. Now, taking a page from the corporate marketing book, you have a product to sell. If you create the best package, best message, and bring it to market in the most effective way, you'll beat the competition. It means putting the very best look and spin on your product, and removing any possible "sales inhibitors"—those little downers like broken this, dirty that, even undisclosed or unresearched information that could turn a buyer away.

Why Is It Important?

Tight competition in a bad market means getting your home to stand out among the others becomes more important than ever. You want to have the best product on the shelf.

What to Do

Think about what's unique and different. Is your home just like all the others around it? Is it just a commodity, like a bushel of corn or a ream of paper? Maybe, but probably not. It always surprises me how sellers fail to note what's unique about their home: the location, the décor, some other feature. In fact, they tend to dwell on what makes it just like other homes: plenty of oak and tile, granite counters, wet bar. Step back, think outside the box, make it as unique and special as possible in a buyer's eyes.

Create a message. Once you've figured out what's unique and different, create a message. Realtors can help, but they have a tendency to create messages that sound like everyone else's. "Cute little charmer in a park-like setting." Think different. Heck, name your home—something clever and creative that reflects something about the home and maybe even you. Mine, a twentieth-century shingle-style Craftsman, is called Shingle Belle.

Make it look perfect. Can't stress this enough: If buyers find imperfections—holes in walls, spots on carpet, weeds in the garden—it gives them a reason not to buy. Hire out a landscape cleanup, use a professional stager (I'm always amazed at what they do).

Get the word out. Many sellers (and realtors) are content to stick a for-sale sign in the ground, post the house on the multiple listing service, and let things happen. Those are all important things to do, but don't rely on an agent and a for-sale sign alone. Let your friends know. Let your network know. Post ads on the company and community bulletin boards. And encourage (and help) your realtor to host as many open houses as possible—people do notice. Even though they may be neighborhood lookie-loos, they have friends and networks, too.

Tip #57: Should You FSBO?

FSBO stands for For Sale By Owner, and it means that you sell your home yourself or with some transactional assistance from an agency like Help-U-Sell or Assist-to-Sell. It isn't for everyone—it takes a lot of work, time, and sometimes money to sell your own home. But the Internet has made it easier to do. You can save the typical 6 percent commission—$12,000–$13,000 on a median-priced American home—which might be the difference between breaking even and taking a loss on the sale.

Why Is It Important?

As discussed, the savings can be important, and in tight times, you may be able to get to market faster and stand out from the crowd. If you have the time, energy, and drive to do it yourself, great, but be careful—it may not work, and you may end up in greater despair and farther behind on your crisis resolution than you would have been otherwise. So make the decision carefully.

What to Do

Check web resources. Sites like *www.forsalebyowner.com* and *www.fsbo.com* can help, as well as the real-estate assist companies mentioned above. Review the how to's and advice on these sites.

Develop a game plan. Really, it's a business plan for bringing your home to market. State a time limit for your FSBO effort. Do your research into your local market using Trulia and Zillow sites mentioned in the sidebar above, and the National Association of Realtors site (*www.realtor.com*). Write down a plan for fixes, price, and how you'll get the word out.

Have lots of open houses. The more you can present your house to the market, the more likely you'll link up to a potential buyer— or someone else who knows a buyer. Make it an event, a celebration, a party, within reason. You need the exposure, and the thousands you'll save will more than compensate for the time. Personally I've sold two homes FSBO after a single open house in moderately soft markets.

Get the word out. As mentioned in Tip #56 about marketing, it's all about getting the word out. Friends, family, colleagues, neighbors, relocation specialists, and realtors all count, as well as any professional or social networks you might be part of. Some FSBO websites make it easy to create your own webpage and even your own MLS listing for your home. (Example: *www.ListbyOwner onMls.com.*)

Don't let realtors talk you out of it. You'll get proposals from realtors to list your home, replete with reasons why only their way

works. If they come to you saying they have a buyer, look out—
they may just be trying for your listing—the buyer doesn't really
exist. So stand your ground, but at the same time, don't alienate
them. If your FSBO doesn't work in a stated period of time—
maybe a month or two—engage a realtor.

Tip #58: Not a Borrower, but a Renter Be

You've been told for years that owning your own home was the
American Dream, and it became almost a matter of public policy
during the 2005–2006 real-estate boom. Almost 70 percent of
U.S. households owned their own homes. But should that have
happened? Could such a high percentage own? Should they own,
given their situations and needs? The answer was apparently no.
Home ownership makes sense for a lot of folks, but it's hardly a
dividing line between success and failure.

Why Is It Important?

At all times in your life you need to make prudent family and
financial decisions; decisions that balance benefits and costs, risk
and reward. In a downturn, the decisions you make are especially
important, as staying out of trouble becomes more important than
enjoying an expanded lifestyle. And it's more important than bowing to peer pressure and following the crowd—in fact, during the
last downturn, it suddenly became hip to rent. It's important to
realistically assess whether you should own or rent.

What to Do

Guess how long you'll stay where you are. Of course, the rent-ver-
sus-buy decision depends on the cost of each and what you think
will happen with your income. Stability is the advantage of ownership—that is, your housing cost is nearly fixed over time. If you
stay in the home for years, owning may make sense. If you antici-

pate moves—for career, economic, or personal reasons, renting works better.

Estimate your rent-to-value ratio. To help decide whether renting makes sense, put yourself in the landlord's shoes. Now, if you own a property worth $400,000 (market value) that fetches $1,000 a month rent, that seems pretty good, right? Well, not really. One thousand dollars a month is $12,000 a year. As a return on investment, $12,000 divided by $400,000 is 3 percent. Clearly, the investor would be better off investing somewhere else—especially after other expenses are considered. But it may be a good deal for you! Such a property would have to rent for twice that much to achieve a decent 6 percent return. So, $1,000 isn't so bad—you're better off being a renter than the owner! It's a handy way to think about it.

Offer to help around the house. If times are really tight for you and you're an experienced homeowner, you might save some rent money by offering to do tasks, fix ups, etc., for the landlord in lieu of rent. It doesn't hurt to ask.

Rehab your credit. If you've faced a housing crisis and have abandoned homeownership, a rental period is a perfect time to build or rebuild your credit. You'll do a lot better next time around in the housing market if your score is above 700, still better if above 740.

Tip #59: Or Is It the Time to Buy?

When times are tough, most of us pull the sheets over our heads and try to hide until the storm passes. Aside from the risks of ignoring obvious messages like delinquent notices and other bills, it might work. Who wants to watch their stocks tank month after month, anyway?

But time and time again, downturns prove to be good times to buy, if you have the stomach and wherewithal to do it. Demand is low, supply's high, people are praying for a qualified buyer to come along, and may take any price to sell it. "It" can be a home, but also a vehicle, a boat, etc.

Why Is It Important?

Downturn means a buyer's market, and if you've played your cards right, you can get great deals. When in a financial funk, it's common to only think about the bad side. If you decide to or are forced to sell a home at an unfavorable price, that's bad. But don't forget, you may be able to buy something cheap if the cards line up right.

What to Do

Find the bottom of your market. It can be hard to do, but try to discover just how much cheap homes or other coveted assets are getting. With homes, talk to realtors or go to some open houses for foreclosures. Judge the activity. I once watched almost forty people stream through a bargain foreclosure open house. Eleven offers were written and it ended up selling for 10 percent over the asking price. Good chance that selling price was a bottom or pretty close to it.

Up, down, or sideways? It's not just where a market is, it's where it's been and where it's going. Get data from Trulia or a real-estate professional. And be careful to compare apples to apples and get specific data for the neighborhood (or among similar neighborhoods) you have in mind—metro-area averages can frequently be misleading.

Talk to lenders before you look. You want to have your "number" in mind before you shop, and you want to know if lenders will back you and for how much. That makes you a stronger buyer.

Be a quiet, strong buyer. Especially in a weak market, as buyer you're king. They'll roll out the red carpet. Be nice, be courteous, but don't tip your hand or rush into anything. Take advantage of your advantage, but don't let it turn into arrogance. Remember, as bad off as a seller might be, they don't want to lose to you.

Tip #60: BK If You Must

BK doesn't stand for Burger King. It's financial lingo for bankruptcy, and it can deal a "whopper" to one's personal finances for years. But under the right circumstances, it can also delay or get you out of a foreclosure. A Chapter 7 bankruptcy allows you to discharge all debts, but the Bankruptcy Reform Act of 2005 makes that harder to do, requiring expensive and time-consuming proof that you indeed need this protection. Chapter 13, which requires a restructuring of debts, not a discharge, is more common.

Why Is It Important?

Both forms of bankruptcy can eliminate or delay a foreclosure; however, bankruptcy should only be undertaken when the rest of your financial picture is hopeless, not just the home. If it's just the home, the workout option, or a straight foreclosure, is usually best. BK may be more helpful if there are multiple loans on the property.

A BK remains on your credit report for ten years and will adversely affect a broader range of credit activity—it's the worst hit possible to your credit. If you're hopelessly behind on most other debts or have a large unexpected expense like a hospital bill or a chronic income problem, BK can make sense. But you must act and decide quickly, for once a home is in the Notice of Sale stage, BK won't help.

What to Do

Get credit counseling. Mortgage counseling will help, but since the problem likely extends beyond housing cost, a broader look makes sense—and will probably be required in bankruptcy court. Counselors can advise whether BK makes sense, and may also recommend so-called *debt settlement* as a way to reduce other debts. It's important to find an honest and accredited nonprofit counselor; check out the National Foundation for Credit Counseling (*www.nfcc.org*), the Association of Independent Consumer Credit

Counseling Agencies (*www.aiccca.org*), or the Department of Justice list of approved credit-counseling agencies (*www.usdoj.gov/ust/ eo/bapcpa/ccde/cc_approved.htm*).

Review with a bankruptcy attorney. If BK does look likely, engage an attorney. You'll need to know the specifics of how Federal and state law apply to your situation, and you'll probably appear in court eventually.

Keep excellent records. Like workouts, bankruptcy is complicated, and you'll get the best results if you have clear records of what you have, what you owe, income, expenses, etc. Keep track of everything, including correspondence.

Say what you're going to do, do what you say. Bankruptcy may wipe the slate clean or give you more favorable terms to help you recover, but it will blow up quickly if you get into—or back into— bad habits. Take it seriously and do the best you can to make it a win-win for you and your creditors.

Tip #61: Navigate the Grief Cycle

You're having a personal housing crisis, and you're about to take a financial and emotional hit if you haven't already. As mentioned at the chapter outset, it's important to put the whole thing in perspective. Homeownership is like any other relationship, and its abrupt and unwelcome termination can deal you a blow not unlike losing a loved one. But it's only a home, not your life; it's only money, not your life. I believe that understanding the grief cycle and its stages will help you cope and come out the other end stronger.

Why Is It Important?

Navigating any crisis requires staying focused and rational, not letting emotions take over. That means realizing that it isn't just about you, and being able to step back to realize that certain reactions are natural. The sooner you can get through the grief cycle and get your financial life back on track, the better.

What to Do

Denial. This is the dangerous stage where mail doesn't get opened; the problem is ignored in the false hope that it might go away. It will get worse. Recognize the phase and move on.

Anger. Also dangerous. You want to fight with your lender, pick nits, stall, blow up, call him a crook, demand assistance. Doesn't work. Get through this stage as soon as possible, too. Remember, win-win works best.

Bargaining. And now we look for the win-win. You bargain with yourself, your lender, your family, others. You look for ways to justify what you did and ways to make yourself whole by promising where you intend to go. Some of these promises work, some don't—be prepared for setbacks. Focus your energy on bargaining with lenders and creditors, not justifying yourself in your own eyes or dwelling on the what-ifs.

Depression. You're likely to be a little depressed from the beginning, and slip back into gloomy mode when various bargaining efforts don't work. You may go back and forth between these stages a few times. It's hard, but you must sweep the feelings aside and keep the energy strong and positive, else despair sets in and loss is more likely and more enduring.

Acceptance. Once you work out the deal with your lender, or sell or lose the house and move on, realize that it's just an event. Your dog or cat still loves you, your children are still growing up, and all of that. And you've learned something from experience that will help the next time around.

Part III

Hold On to Your Lifestyle

Chapter 8

Financial Forensics

Where does the money go? Whether the economy sucks or not, effective personal finance starts with answering this question. Life happens fast, and the average family spends its money on dozens—hundreds—of things, some large and some small. We all know from experience that large things are important. We also know that small things can add up to a large number in a hurry.

The whole idea, downturn or not, is to gain control of our finances: control, not for control's sake, but so that we can make sound and effective financial decisions, so we can be efficient with our money. It becomes more important when the economy sucks because it's usually then we feel the most pain; it's usually then that income suffers (and sometimes, costs increase), putting us in a bind—a bind that can cause lasting pain if untended to, but that can usually be made less painful if we stand up and do something about it.

The first part of gaining financial control is to figure out where we are and what we do financially. Without that knowledge, it's hard to proceed on any kind of plan of action, or even get an agreement on what to do. Earlier in this book, I offered the Katherine Neville quote from her novel *The Eight*: "What can be measured can be understood, what can be understood can be altered." No phrase could better describe one's finances, and this chapter covers the "what can be measured can be understood" part.

So what do I mean by financial forensics? Forensics is a scientific exercise of laying out what happened and why after an event occurs. The word "forensics" usually connects to legal events, but the phrase expands well to fit financial events, too.

Financial forensics analyzes:

✔ What was
✔ What is
✔ What changed

This chapter aims the forensic discussion at your ordinary income and expenses; that is, where your money comes from and where it goes. The next chapter explains what to do with that information; that is, how to bring control to your finances to weather a financial storm.

Tip #62: Get Out the Magnifying Glass

The first step is to take a close look at what goes into and what goes out of your financial "house." For a period of time, watch and document—carefully and closely—all income, especially the expense items. Put it on paper or in a spreadsheet. You could also use one of the popular personal financial programs like Quicken or Microsoft Money, but I feel those programs bring too much complexity and distraction to the exercise. At this stage, you're simply tracking your income and expenses, period. It doesn't take long, and you'll learn a lot.

Why Is It Important?

This might be hard to do, especially during a downturn. You may be taking a look-the-other-way approach to managing your finances: it'll all go away, it'll get better, it isn't as bad as it seems. But it's more important now than ever. You may be able to turn your financial ship without drastic measures. You may be able to cut unnecessary expenses to match your income—whether steady or declining. But without financial forensics, you'll never know.

What to Do

Create a positive environment. You recognize a need to get a handle on your finances, but that doesn't mean everyone else will. Approach the exercise diplomatically, with plenty of open communication and family meetings. Explain why it's important and what you're going to do with the information (which is laid out in this and the next chapter). It's a team effort, and the end result will be something for everyone—financial peace, financial reward.

No classified expenses. It's common for family members to avoid disclosing certain expenses for fear of reprisal or ridicule. Financial forensics only works when everything is put on the table. No sacred cows. Otherwise, everyone will have sacred cows—and you'll get nowhere.

Honest answers only. In the same vein, you do yourself no good if you omit or understate certain expenses, or understate income. You won't get to where you want to go.

Decide on a time period. It's a bit of work to collect the data, tedious, some might say, so don't do it for months and months—you need to move forward faster than that, anyway. Two or three weeks might do for the small stuff, maybe a month. You'll probably have to look backward and forward—forward for the undocumented stuff like magazines and lattes, backward is okay for checks you write or stuff on your credit cards. You, or whoever is most knowledgeable about family finances, should take a longer look at those monthly, quarterly, or annual expenses like insurance, property taxes, and gifts.

Tip #63: Categorize Your Spending

Once the list of expenses is put together, you'll need to categorize them as outlined below (or in other ways, as you see fit).

Why Is It Important?

Putting expenses into categories helps you understand them, which in turn helps you decide what to do with them, to manage them. Without this, the list can get a bit overwhelming.

What to Do

Divide it into regular and irregular. Some expenses occur every month—food, rent, utilities. Others show up once in a blue moon, like insurance bills, tax bills, memberships, car license fees, and so forth. A poor understanding of irregular expenses can turn them into budget bombs, as further described below.

Planned and unplanned. Planned and unplanned expenses can be similarly divided. Even though most insurance bills are irregular, you can predict them. You can't predict the $1,500 for the new heater core in your old Volvo. So see how much you incur in unplanned expenses each year; it'll help you build a budget around this amount.

Rising and falling. It's not just about where the puck is, it's about where the puck is going. An expense that's rising (like gas and food in 2008) has different implications than one that's staying the same or falling.

Fixed and discretionary. We'll get back to this in a minute, but some expenses are completely controllable, some are only moderately controllable, and some can't be controlled at all, aside from a major lifestyle change. The difference will become clearer in Tip #66.

Tip #64: Know Your Income Flow

If you and your spouse have regular jobs, you can probably move on to the next tip. But if you're like more and more Americans, self-employed, freelancing, doing extra work on the side, or paid some kind of commission or bonus, income can be as irregular as expenses, if not more so.

Why Is It Important?

As a book author, in some years I've only been paid three or four times—so it's a challenge to make the income cover the dry periods. Unplanned expenses and budget bombs can throw you off track, but so does a poor understanding—and forecast—of income flows. Income can be even more unpredictable than expenses.

What to Do

Ordinary wage earner? You don't have much to worry about. This also applies to regular entitlement earners like retirees—Social Security, pensions, required IRA/401(k) withdrawals, etc.

Meet the commission and bonus challenge. If you're in sales or in a position with significant year-end bonuses or profit sharing, it's important to note past income patterns and plan for the future—likely with a downturn in these income streams. Especially for bonuses, sound financial management in good times may mean socking them away as savings while depending on ordinary income. In a downturn, you may become more dependent on a bonus just as it goes away. Be realistic.

Self-employed, business owners beware. There's hardly anything more variable in personal finance than self-employment or business income—it goes all over the place according to business level, expenses, and how customers and clients pay.

Count investment income, too. Especially if you're retired or otherwise living off of investments, it's important to measure this income, and if it's dividends on stocks, to understand the risks. Many companies cut dividends during the 2007–2008 downturn.

Do scenarios. It helps to do multiple scenarios—high, medium, and low—for all parts of a budget or financial plan. Unless you're a regular wage earner, it's especially important for income planning because it's natural to guess toward the high side.

Tip #65: Debt Is Just a Way to Pay for Something

I've seen or heard it a million times: "Gotta budget $300 a month for my VISA, $100 a month for my MasterCard, and $200 a month for my AMEX."

Well, indeed, you do. You need to make these payments, and so you'll have to put them into your budget at least in the short term until these debts are gone. But what's wrong with this picture? You're just paying off the debt, while not meeting or dealing with the expenses that produced the debt in the first place.

Why Is It Important?

Debt payment is a cash transaction, and yes, you need to make room for it in your budget. But it doesn't get to the heart of your financial enterprise—matching income and expenses. So no, don't ignore debt; that's an incredibly bad idea, especially during a downturn. But recognize it for what it is—a way to pay for some thing, not an expense in and of itself.

What to Do

Watch for the canary in the coal mine. For those of you born since 1960 or who didn't grow up in West Virginia, miners used to put a canary down into a mine shaft. If it stopped singing and died, that was a clear, quick indicator that there wasn't enough oxygen to survive. Debt is the dead canary in your financial coal mine. With some exceptions noted below, when income falls short of expenses, debt is the result. In a downturn, a rise in debt can be the first sign of trouble.

It's the spending, stupid. Want to get your financial house in order? Sure, pay off your debt if you can, but the real secret is to manage your underlying expenses; then you won't have debt!

Take debt payments off the top. In the budgeting process, as described in the next chapter, debt payoff should be taken off the top of your income—before other expenses are budgeted for and met. That way, your income available to meet expenses each month is matched against your true expenses, not mixed in with debts that occurred in prior months.

Recognize good debt and bad debt. Not all debt is bad. Debt used to acquire long-term assets or assets that should rise in value, like real estate, can be considered good debt. So can debt used to acquire something at a very favorable price you would have bought anyway. Bad debt is debt incurred for something consumed and gone before you even make the payment. Car loans and other intermediate installment debt is somewhere in between.

Don't forget interest expenses, fees. There's the debt itself, which you must pay off eventually, but don't forget to tally monthly interest expense and other fees in your expense list.

THE DIFFERENCE BETWEEN DEBT AND CREDIT

Most people closely associate debt and credit, and some assume they're the same thing. Really, they're two sides—a bad side and a good side—of the same coin. Debt is a liability, something you owe. Credit—to the extent it hasn't already been used to take on debt—is an asset, something you earn and own. If you have credit, you have the capability to take on debt to buy something. A capability is a good thing to have, even a better thing when economic times are tough. Get rid of some debt, and your credit will improve.

Tip #66: Get a Grip on the Latte Factor

The latte factor? I first saw the term used with great effect by personal finance author David Bach, of *Automatic Millionaire* fame. It's a nice metaphor for all the things you spend money on that seem small but add up—to a lot.

Why Is It Important?

If you can get a handle on your latte expenses—how much, how often, what they really cost—you can rein in costs while still meeting your financial goals and enjoying most of the good things in life. Lattes tend to be bad habits that largely escape notice. Part of the exercise is not only identifying the lattes, but also knowing what they really cost, especially in the long run.

I have nothing against lattes or other coffeehouse perks, per se. You work hard, I work hard, we all should get a chance to enjoy life's little pleasures and luxuries once in a while. In fact, they can help control the urge to enjoy and spend on bigger ones. So, nothing against Starbucks; it's the metaphor that counts.

What to Do

Money burns holes in pockets. It's inevitable—put a few crisp bills in your pocket, you'll feel rich and spend it easier. (Plastic works this way for some, too—know thy behaviors!) So one savings tactic is to not put money in your pocket. The other is to know where it goes when you do.

Figure it over one year, twenty or thirty years. Spend $4 on a latte per day, save a few weekends—that's $100 a month, or $1,200 per year. And financial compounding formulas tell us, if we set it aside instead of spending it, it could be worth a lot more in twenty or thirty years. At 6 percent, it adds up to $46,204 after twenty years and $100,451 at the end of thirty years. Hardly pocket change anymore.

Is plain coffee good enough? Metaphorically, lattes represent that $2, $3, $10, etc., thing you just don't seem to be able to do without—or that seems small enough to not matter. It helps to not buy those things. It also helps to look for less expensive things that give nearly the same pleasure: coffee, instead of a latte; soda, instead of an $8 glass of wine in a restaurant (the soda's refillable, too). Okay, this moves away from identifying lattes and into strategies for saving money, but it's never too early to start.

Get it into sight, into mind. Some people let too many lattes into their life without even knowing it. Impulse buys at the grocery checkout, VIP parking, product add-ons. Why shop all over town for the cheapest gas, then spend $1.69 on a soda and $3.79 on a bag of chips? Bad habits, that's why.

Tip #67: Line Those Expenses Up Against a Wall

And shoot them? Well, not quite, at least not yet. But now it's time, once again, to classify them yet another way, a way that helps you manage them. In Tip #63 "Categorize Your Spending," we classified expenses by type to get a better understanding of their nature and where they come from. In this exercise, we classify expenses by what we can do about them.

Why Is It Important?

Some expenses are more controllable than others. When you break them into groups according to their controllability, you can take action on them now and in the budgeting process. If your goal is to reduce expenses, concentrate first on the discretionary items, then on the necessities.

What to Do

Obligations. These are the expenses that are fixed and not controllable in the short term, like a mortgage payment, taxes, insurance premiums, and car payments. As they can only be changed by a longer-term change in lifestyle, like moving or a major downsizing, you must make room for them in your expense planning and budgeting. No exceptions!

Necessities. Necessities are also musts, but you have at least some control over how much you spend on them. Food or utilities must all be bought in a given month, but you have some control over what kind of food, how much food, how much electricity, how much driving, and so forth. Home improvements and similar expenses also fall into this group. They must be in your budget, but you can control the how much part by choice and family agreement. Be creative.

Discretionary items. These items are strictly a matter of choice— entertainment, eating out, books, magazines, CDs, iTunes downloads, probably even cell phones. You have lots of control; there are lots of tradeoffs.

Tip #68: Find Your Budget Bombs

You're sailing along through the month, money in the checking account, most bills paid, kids' allowances taken care of. Then the old Volvo radiator breaks. Then there's your sister's wedding, with $200 for the gift and a weekend trip. And your buddies decide this is golf week, so a $100 round of golf, $20 off the beverage cart, and dinner. Your best-laid plans bite the dust.

Why Is It Important?

Budget bombs happen. The best way to deal with them is to see them coming and either avoid them or recognize and plan for their impact. Some, like the $800 weekend, are worth doing once in a while—but people tend to underestimate the total cost and impact on finances, and once the bombs hit, they usually turn into debt—causing financial destruction for some time to come.

What to Do

Following are some examples—but not a complete list—of bombs.

Car repairs, medical bills, insurance bills. Most car repairs are unforeseen, but they happen, they're expensive, and they must be dealt with, preferably with some form of rainy-day fund. Doctor bills, dentist bills—you get the idea. Insurance bills sneak up on you because you aren't used to paying them every month.

Gifts, holidays. Some gift purchases are unpredictable, like a wedding or a thank-you gift. Others happen every year—like birthdays and Christmas—yet people just don't plan for them. So, onto the credit cards they go.

The $800 weekend. Two bargain $99 air fares, two bargain nights in a hotel, a $150 rental car tab, meals, airport parking—all sound like good deals when you shop them—they probably are, but they add up. You must stay aware of the total cost, not just how cheap each item is individually.

Small stuff. The list is endless—interest charges, fees, overdrafts, junk and "gotcha" charges on credit cards, phones, banks, cable/satellite TV—it can add up to hundreds. Much of it is avoidable, often with a simple phone call to the provider. These costs are small enough and numerous enough it's hard to even track or budget for them, but you'll be surprised at how much you can do about them. See Bob Sullivan's excellent *Gotcha Capitalism: How Hidden Fees Rip You Off Every Day and What You Can Do About Them* (Ballantine, 2007) for more.

Tip #69: Look Under Other Rocks

As you do financial forensics, there's no telling what you'll discover. Some items will be quite familiar, like your mortgage or rent payment. Some may be uncomfortable, like amounts spent for the comfort and joy of a particular family member. Some will be total surprises, the "ahas" that make it all worthwhile.

Why Is It Important?

There's no sense starving yourself or freezing in winter if you're throwing cash away, say, on a dial-up connection or a paging service you never use. As they say in the corporate world, go after the low-hanging fruit first. It's easiest, and may save a bigger lifestyle shakedown to survive a downturn.

What to Do

Plan entertainment and refreshments. You never know when your buddies will get something together, and yes, you shouldn't avoid them all the time just in the interest of saving cash. But it's easy for a casual and well-planned evening at a restaurant to get out of control, too—an $8 glass of wine, two $7 glasses of beer, a $9 dessert. Amazing how two $20 entrees turn into a $120 tab, right? Do it a few times a month, and it's real money.

Find stuff you don't use. Or use enough. It happens all the time—we buy it, sign up for it, don't use it. Premium cable/satellite channels, movie packages, additional receivers, gym memberships, old dial-up connections, storage units, maintenance or service agreements for an old product or something you don't even have anymore. This isn't the government—cut the crap.

Watch out for statement misstatements. I'm a seasoned personal finance type with a graduate business degree and well connected to the ins and outs of my finances. But can I read my electric bill? Phone bill? Health explanation-of-benefits statement? Bank or credit card statement? Barely, if at all. And they're loaded with surprises, some you can cut, like the $6 a month "protection plan" for your satellite receiver (which would almost buy a replacement in a year). Learn to read your statements, and for any doubts, have an agent walk you through it over the phone.

Automatic billings and withdrawals. It's another out of sight, out of mind factor. People sign up for things and have them turned into automatic checking account withdrawals or credit card billings. It's simple, and the seller pushes it because you won't have to think about writing that check, and they get their money sooner. Look at your statements for wine programs, computer game subscriptions, life insurance, charitable contributions. Online banking and bill pay make these easier to track, too.

Tip #70: Don't Expose Yourself

We're not talking about clothing, or lack thereof, created in the interest of saving money. We're talking about keeping you and family members away from spending traps—places and images designed, calculated to get you to buy something. Resistance and discipline are important.

Why Is It Important?

Marketers have applied a hundred years of science and experience toward separating you from your money, and they're pretty good at it. And certain behaviors and habits of your own, if not checked, tend to cause unnecessary spending. It's important to recognize these outside and inside stimuli and be able to respond to them with a straight face and a closed wallet.

What to Do

Know the effects of advertising. We're bombarded with advertising, 24/7 (well, almost) in every medium from newspapers and magazines to TV, radio, and the Internet. Resist temptation.

Just because it's cheap doesn't mean you need it. "Hey, that pair of shoes is normally $150, and it's only $99.99." Do you need it? Probably not. And buying something used or on eBay or at a garage sale is no bargain, either, if you don't need it. The other side of that coin, of course, is if you *do* need it, go right ahead, and it may even justify using credit to buy it.

If you don't need to shop, don't. For a lot of people, shopping is a way to get out of the summer doldrums or winter blues. That's okay, but recognize that every shopping trip brings a risk to your finances, especially when times are tight. For me, my most enjoyable shopping trips happen when I don't buy anything (see what I *saved?*) but I might enjoy a nice ice cream cone or get an idea for something I can make along the way.

Avoid Pandora's boxes. Ah yes—we splurged and bought ski passes for everyone this year. Very nice. Now what about new skis, a new outfit, new gloves, new goggles? Might as well go all the way, right? Not right. Just because the family embarks on a new adventure or a new year doesn't mean everything's fair game. One step at a time. Why, we just paid for the ski passes—lighten up, everyone! Watch out for that everything-goes mentality when you or the family starts something new.

The high price of hitting the road. Travel almost always costs more than we think it will. Most travel is bought piecemeal, not in packages, and it adds up. You're paying your living expenses, and then some, along the way. Remember, your original living expenses at home don't stop, so always be realistic and plan ahead for travel. One of the worst financial traps is paying debt for months or years for a trip that's a long-distant memory. Of course, you need to get away once in a while, and of course there are valuable family experiences, but keep it all in perspective and within the confines of your resources.

Chapter 9

Should You Live on a Budget?

Budget. No matter how you say the word, it sounds bad, ominous. It brings connotations of discipline, control, lack of choice, responsibility. You don't have these things, so you need a budget. On top of that, there's lots of detailed record keeping—being called on the carpet to answer and justify every dime spent.

Taken together, it's not a very positive image. And when the economy sucks, all you need right now is more bad news about your own personal economy. It's like hearing you've gained weight, can't eat anymore, and have to switch to big and tall clothing. Bad message on top of bad message—yuck.

So I'm here to tell you about a different approach to the word "budget" and all the things it means. It doesn't have to be as bad as it sounds. If you follow my budgeting principles, where "living on a budget" becomes more of a way of life than a numbers-based mandate, you may find that it actually works.

First, a word about goals. Financial advisers talk a lot about goals, and a lot of that talk is overrated. But when it comes to budgeting, it helps to start with the end in mind, especially in a down economy where the need to budget isn't a matter of choice. The ultimate goal during a downturn is to spend less, because you know your income isn't going up anytime soon. Worse, some key ingredients to your life might be getting more expensive, as gasoline did in 2007–2008. It's a matter of making it all fit, and a 10 percent drop in expenses works just the same as—or even better than—a 10 percent raise! (Why? Think taxes.)

Back to the Katherine Neville mantra: "What can be measured can be understood, what can be understood can be altered." The last chapter covered the "what can be measured can be understood"; this chapter covers the "what can be understood can be altered" part. I'll share painless ways to adopt a budget mentality, get it done, and get family members to follow and support it.

Many of the principles outlined here can be explored further in another of my books (done with my wife Jennifer) called *The Pocket Idiot's Guide to Living on a Budget 2nd ed.* (Alpha Books, 2007).

Tip #71: Know Why Most Budgets Fail

Perhaps you've tried it before; laid out a detailed spending plan for you and each and every family member to follow, but it met the usual fate—it didn't get followed. When you sat down with family members to ask why, they simply crawled into a shell, or worse, got mad, and it all fell apart. Why is budgeting so hard, and why does it not only not work, but sometimes cause unintended consequences, like extra spending, family discord, even divorce?

Why Is It Important?

Very simple: Budgets that don't work are worse than worthless, because of the anxiety and contempt they can breed.

What to Do

Failure to understand the goal. The goal of the budgeting process is not to get control over family members or put a lid on spending; it is to learn about our finances and make rational choices and get us through a tough period as a team. Or something like that.

Failure to understand the facts. "Garbage in, garbage out," the old mantra from the dawn of the computer age, also applies to budgeting. If you don't do your homework, that number you come up with for what the family can spend on, say, entertainment doesn't mean much and probably won't be adhered to. Make sure to do the financial forensics first.

The power and control thing. Power and control, where one family member takes charge of the budget and tells everyone else what they can and can't do, kills more budgets than anything else. When people lose autonomy and choice, when their authority is separated from their responsibility, bad things happen. Do your budgeting in a participative, open-faced environment, where everyone shares in the decision, commitment, and ultimate reward.

Lack of discipline. The sheer inability to stick to a commitment is also a budget killer. Make sure everyone buys into the idea and the need to get through the downturn.

"How's it gonna benefit me?" When family members feel no benefit from going into budget mode, the budget is at risk. Be clear how each family member will benefit (a clear allowance, discussed below), that there will be more for everyone when things improve, and there is some kind of reward for everyone who sticks to the script (also discussed next).

Tip #72: Find the Smart Budgeting Premise—and Promise

Budgeting doesn't have to be a burdensome, detailed process put forth as numbers handed down from above. It can be streamlined into a few important numbers to follow, decided on and implemented as a team, and supported by rewards for a job well done. Everyone wins now, everyone wins more when the economy gets better.

So smart budgeting is a shared effort, based on facts, and aligned to monitoring a few key numbers with individual flexibility and freedom within those numbers. It's easy to follow, empowers individuals, and rewards good behavior.

Why Is It Important?

Using a smart budget process avoids the why-most-budgets-fail traps.

What to Do

Create shared, agreed-to goals. When times are good, everyone needs to agree on the long-term goals ($X saved for retirement, $Y for that vacation home someday, $Z for new snowboards for the family). When times are tough, it may actually be easier: we need to do this in case a job goes away; to save our home and our lifestyle; to make sure Jimmy still gets to go to college. Make sure everyone in the family knows what the goals are and agrees with them.

Keep authority and responsibility together. Anytime you separate authority and responsibility, you're asking for trouble. People don't want to feel the burden of something, like saving money or taking out the trash, unless they also have some authority for how to save money or when to take out the trash. Smart budgeting gives people autonomy and control, at least within the allowances they receive within the budget plan.

Focus on categories and allowances, not detail. Smart budgeting means avoiding the trap of budgeting every latte, newspaper or magazine, and meal out. It's too much work, too easy to stray from, and when it's strayed from a little, it's usually strayed from a lot. Individual family members will get allowances within which they have total freedom to spend. It simplifies the budget process and allows family members to keep some authority.

Reward good behavior. At the end of a month, a quarter, a downturn, everyone in the family who follows the program gets some kind of reward. It doesn't have to be big—a gift card or something like that. Or if the family pulls through a crisis, maybe it is bigger—a vacation or something like that. Of course, the reward shouldn't be so big that it throws the family back into crisis!

Tip #73: PYF

PYF stands for Pay Yourself First. No, this isn't about you as a business owner paying yourself a fat salary before paying your workers. It's about you as a family or household unit setting aside money for important stuff off the top of your paycheck, into some form of savings or rainy-day fund aligned to your goals and financial security.

Why Is It Important?

As we all know, money available to spend gets spent. So if all of our take-home pay ends up in the checking account, with a checkbook and perhaps several debit cards to access it, that money burns a hole in the proverbial pocket. By setting money aside and ahead of ordinary expenses, we build up the reserves, financial security, and savings for any number of goals, including retirement, college, health care, or the boat everyone wants.

In times of financial crisis, it may be too late to do PYF, but it's an excellent strategy if you're still healthy and anticipating trouble, and always good to the extent you can afford it.

What to Do

Save for what-if—the rainy-day fund. So how do you cover that unexpected car repair or dental crown, anyway? It's by setting aside a rainy-day fund, a fund to handle the unexpected. Without such a fund, those expenses will likely turn into debt. This fund may be comingled with the emergency fund discussed in Chapter 1, but that fund is more to cover income shortfalls than unexpected expenses.

Save for goals. Separate PYF accounts cover savings for retirement, big purchases, college, etc. Funds should be transferred automatically, and as reasonable, from your payroll directly into these accounts. For retirement, 10 percent of gross income is an ambitious goal, but will lead to a healthy golden age. You can base any of these savings amounts on percent of income, actual need, or a fixed number of dollars.

Save for debt relief. If you have debt already, the payoff should come from a PYF transfer, not be part of your expense budget. Debt shouldn't be considered a budget expense—it's a way you paid for some other, previous expense.

Take care of irregular expenses. Smart budgeters set up yet another PYF arrangement for those irregular expenses like insurance premiums or property tax payments. It's similar to the impound accounts you may have for property tax and homeowners' insurance, but you keep control and earn the interest, not the escrow company.

Tip #74: Pay Yourselves an Allowance

When you were eleven or twelve—maybe younger, maybe older—your parents gave you a weekly allowance. You could spend it however you pleased. Didn't you feel empowered? Regardless of how big the allowance was, the important part was that you had the control of the money.

The same practice can apply to grownup budgeting. Give each spouse an allowance—say, $300 a month—to be spent however they want. New clothes, lattes, magazines, eBay purchases—doesn't matter. You can give them an individual debit or credit card to make these purchases with—all the better to keep track.

Why Is It Important?

Allowances give personal flexibility and control while still keeping to a spending limit.

What to Do

Create a family allowance. The family allowance is just as it sounds—an amount set aside for all family purposes, which can range from movies and entertainment to planting a garden or other home improvements or even vacations, depending on how defined. The family must agree on expenses, and again, a separate credit card helps track. By the way, I've used Discover cards for years for family allowances because the cash back bonuses are another worthwhile reward.

Allocate personal allowances, or PALs. As laid out above, each family member gets an allowance decided upon as the budget is decided upon. Once the number's in place—no more questions—do whatever you want. Unused allowance amounts, like cell phone minutes, can be saved for another month.

Taschengeld. From growing up in an ethnic German family, this word translates to "pocket money." In addition to an allowance, each family member can get an additional pocket-money allowance for really small stuff—a soda here, a bus fare there. It equates to petty cash in the corporate world and to ATM withdrawals for many individuals. So give everyone (or at least the adults) a $40 Taschengeld ATM withdrawal each week.

Tip #75: File Those Expenses Under . . .

In the last chapter we sliced and diced your expenses into a lot of different categories to understand their nature, where they come from, and how easy they'll be to control. Now it's time to do a budget worksheet. However you decide to lay it out—this is where the expenses are laid out, and where income resources are allocated to them. It is here where the budget premise and promise meet the road.

Why Is It Important?

What can be understood can be altered—and here is where you start altering it. The budget will become your basic tool for coping with difficult times, and you can alter and amend it as you need to if the situation gets worse or, with luck, if it gets better.

What to Do

Develop the worksheet. It doesn't matter how you do this. Back of a napkin is okay, a PC spreadsheet may be better because you can make changes easily. But PC stuff may intimidate some family members and be a tad too formal. Your choice.

Categorize expenses. Lay out your expenses—obligations, necessities, discretionary—as assigned in Tip #63. For more on how this works, refer to *The Pocket Idiot's Guide to Living on a Budget*.

Learn what months to watch out for. If you haven't done this already, figure out which months are the toughest—when insurance bills come in, homeowners' association dues are payable, December holidays. Pay particular attention to those periods.

Drop those budget bombs. As a first cut, figure out ways to eliminate or deal with budget bombs (see Tip #68). For the budget bombs you can't get rid of, figure out a PYF amount to put into each month's budget to take care of them.

Tip #76: Match Income and Expenses

The point is to construct a numbers-based and doable budget matching expenses, allowances, and the income to meet them. The detail is beyond scope here, but can be found in *The Pocket Idiot's Guide to Living on a Budget.*

In this step, you've already laid out the expenses, now you match your income with the expenses, starting with the highest priorities, including PYF amounts, and working down into the lowest-priority discretionary items.

Why Is It Important?

It isn't real if it isn't methodical, and it isn't real if there isn't enough money to do what you want or need to do. This process allocates your income and rebalances and reworks it if (when!) things come up short.

What to Do

Figure your net pay. The first step—and you've probably done this—is to figure out your net pay. Where this is more difficult is if you have income from sources other than employment—a business, self-employment, investments, etc. Be realistic about what you really bring home.

PYF. As the PYF acronym implies (see Tip #73), you then allocate income to PYF items. Okay, so Uncle Sam and your state get paid before you do; get over it.

What's available. So-called take-home pay won't really be take-home if you've set up proper PYF amounts. So net less PYF is what's really available to meet monthly bills and for spending.

What's spendable. The next step is to deduct obligations (from Chapter 8 Tip #67). You can't control these costs, and you can't spend that money on anything else. So once deducted, the remaining amount is spendable—you have some control over how and how much of it is spent.

What's discretionary. You just figured spendable income, but you still have some pretty tall needs like food and home maintenance that require monthly spending. These *necessities* can be controlled, to a degree. Take an estimated amount away—the remainder is discretionary; that is, it can be spent as you and the family please, including allowance amounts.

Find the net net. Finally, after discretionary expenses are allocated, you have your bottom line. It's a pretty good bet this amount is negative—especially in tough times. That's okay, don't despair, it's normal. You simply have to go back and make things balance. And if your number does happen to be positive, increase your PYF or other savings amounts.

Balance and rebalance. If at first you don't succeed . . . this final step is where everything gets worked out. Massage and remassage, give and take, do a few different scenarios. This works best when everyone is present and in on the decision. When you get to something everyone can agree on, make a deal, make copies, and get on with the month.

Tip #77: Handle Those Special Situations

Living on a budget will help you understand and deal with the regular stuff pretty well; you'll get into a routine. But life isn't always so regular, right? We've talked about irregular income (Tip #64) and so-called budget bombs (Tip #68), now it's time to talk about how to handle life's little events, surprises, dreams, and desires. These aren't really budget bombs, but things you want to do but need to make sure you've got the money to do.

Why Is It Important?
An effective budget doesn't just cover the have-to stuff; it should also handle the special needs and desires of you and your family.

What to Do

Budget for holiday gifts. Christmas and other gift-giving holidays don't have to be filled with budget bombs. In fact, within your family, they can become part of the reward system. For more than one reason, it helps to plan your gifts in advance, not only to create the proper PYF (sort of like an old-fashioned Christmas Fund once offered by your corner savings and loan), but to reward yourself and others with your new financial providence. You'll find that providing adequately for gifts is extremely rewarding. And how discouraging is it when things aren't adequate? It really becomes a matter of feeling good about yourself.

Life's little events. Graduations, weddings, baby showers—every family has its own, and recognizes such events with friends and others.

Buying big stuff. Okay, during a downturn you probably don't have a big-screen TV on your wish list. But what if you did? What if times weren't so bad? How you handle big stuff can make or break your finances. Too often, we just throw caution to the winds and charge it. That can make sense if it's a really good deal, but even good deals aren't so good if they throw your financials to the alligators. Big stuff should be like any other financial goal, and handled with some kind of PYF fund set up for the purpose. Family agreement is important, and any leftovers from an allowance should go toward it as an incentive to spend that allowance wisely.

Tip #78: Find "Typical" Ways to Save Money

Perhaps you bought this book looking for some immediate ways to save money. So, here is a list.

Why Is It Important?

Living on a budget is important, and these ideas will help make your budget balance. They'll also exercise your creativity and stimulate other, related ideas. Finally, you'll feel good about your frugality and resourcefulness, and it'll become a habit and even fun for you and your family.

What to Do

Increase insurance deductibles. Most people buy too much insurance. Yes, you should cover your life, car, property, health, and disability, but where deductibles are involved, how much insurance do you really need? The difference between a $500 and a $2,000 deductible on homeowners' insurance can be $300 a year. Would you normally pay $300 a year for $1,500 in insurance? Probably not. The more you can self-insure for small stuff, the more you'll save. Insurance should be for the big stuff.

Eat in, don't drink out. As nice as it is to get away from doing dishes, it's expensive to take a family of four to dinner. There's the cost of a full meal and beverage, plus dessert, tax, a 15 percent tip; the latter two add 18–22 percent to a bill by themselves. Then there are the drinks, particularly alcohol. This is where most restaurants make money. I recently had a major "beef" with a large restaurant suburban chain for not publishing the price of a glass of house wine on the menu. After talking to the restaurant manager, I found out it was 7 bucks for a tiny glass. Shame on them for not publishing it—and shame on you if you order glass after glass.

Drive less. With the advent of $4 a gallon gas, it seems kind of obvious, but most people are focused on the gas mileage of their vehicle and "When will this all end?" Whether it does or doesn't, you do control at least some of your driving. There are creative ways to cope: carpool, "trip-pool" (combine trips), put the kids on a school bus, have car-free days once a week. If you cut just 100 miles a week, that's about $20 a week, or over $1,000 a year.

Don't use it—lose it. Make a list of things you aren't using and check it each month. Like the health club, storage unit, or Netflix subscription.

Do it yourself. As a busy but leisure-focused society, we tend to avoid doing mundane tasks like yard work, mowing the lawn, and washing the car and simply pay someone else. When times are tight, think about what you pay others to do and what you could save by doing them yourself. You'll get plenty of exercise, and self-satisfaction from the notion that you did it yourself and did it to survive or achieve some financial goal.

Rent it, don't buy it. Need a pressure washer? The first instinct is to go out and buy one, but maybe you use it twice a year. Try renting instead. Not only will you save the purchase price, but maintenance and obsolescence, too. This can work for anything from party furniture to boats. Check out your local rental yard some day when you don't have much to do.

Buy used. The advent of eBay and craigslist have brought this one back into vogue. Why buy new when you can get something just as good for one-third or even half the price? Buy a one-to-three-year-old car at used-car specialist CarMax, and save one-third to half over the equivalent new car. My wife Jennifer frequents consignment stores, buying anything from Levi's to Chanel for a fraction of the price. It's fun and gives her something to do when she travels.

Tip #79: Payback Time

Nothing ventured, nothing gained. It's no secret that we're a capitalist society, motivated by financial reward for our sacrifices, effort, time, and investments at the end of the day. Living on a budget just because it's the right thing to do might get you somewhere, but might only get you so far if you're asking family members to give something up (which you inevitably will). It helps to have some skin in the game, and a reward serves that premise well.

Why Is It Important?

Rewards are especially important for downturn budgeting. Why? Because things are tight, and everyone's nervous as the storm clouds approach or thicken. A reward promised when the sun shines again can be just the incentive to get everyone singing from the same budgeting hymn book.

What to Do

Find ways to reward your team. Be creative: predetermined gift cards for each member of your family; a massage; dinner; a night on the town; a short trip, or perhaps a long one if the size of the crisis justifies it.

Try a nonfinancial reward. Spend a romantic evening together at home, go for a long walk, or best, make a special gift for one another to celebrate your newfound financial security.

Make it actually work. A reward should be decided on and agreed to in advance. It should be real, tangible, and valuable, but not so much that it throws your finances back into the mud again, of course.

Chapter 10

Smart Debt, Smart Credit

If you had to put your finger on any one resource that has supported the American Way and the standard of living we're all accustomed to, you'd have quite a list of items to choose from. That list would include an assortment of unmatched physical and agricultural resources and a diverse, adaptable human resource.

But there's one other feature—for better or for worse—that has served as the grease to lubricate the wheels and the fertilizer to expand the fields of American consumerism and capitalism: credit. In America, like no other place, it is possible to borrow money for just about anything—a lot of it, and at generally favorable interest rates. And borrow a lot we do. According to the Federal Reserve, as a nation we have some $10 *trillion* in mortgage debt. That's a lot, but it might be considered "good" debt (I'll talk about that in a moment) because it funds an important long-term asset: our homes. Of course, too much is too much, as the 2007–2008 mortgage crisis and the declining value of that long-term asset showed. I'll talk about that, too.

We also have piled on some $2.4 trillion in personal consumer debt, which mostly includes credit cards and installment loans (like car loans). Since that's only one-quarter of the mortgage debt, it doesn't seem like so much, right? But, considered a different way, that's some $8,100 per U.S. citizen, or $21,900 per household. It's about 130 percent of our annual disposable income. And a good bit of it goes for bad debt—debt taken on to buy short-lived consumer products, vacations, entertainment, and other items of questionable long-term value.

Debt Versus Credit: The Very Least You Need to Know

You thought debt and credit were the same thing; use a credit card, you go into debt. No, they aren't the same at all, and in fact the difference is very important to getting a grip on your personal finances, downturn or not. In fact, the following three principles will help you manage credit and debt in good times and bad.

1. Debt is a liability, while credit is an asset.

Debt is what happens after money is actually borrowed. You have to pay it back, with interest. And if you used that money to buy the right kind of thing, it's okay and probably even good. But if the borrowed money is simply spent with no lasting value, the money is gone and so is the purchase, but the debt is still on your books. In accounting- and personal finance-speak, debt is a liability.

Credit, on the other hand, is the *potential* to borrow money. If you have a lot of credit but don't have much debt, that means lenders are willing to lend you money to buy. But you haven't used the privilege, it's still in the future should you decide to do it. So credit is an *asset*, and it's something you should take care of, manage, like an asset.

So, credit is good, debt is bad.

2. Asset values may decline, but debt values don't (unless paid off).

As a nation, we discovered this big time in the 2007–2008 downturn. Home prices softened, but the value of the debt used to buy homes—mortgages—didn't change. The result: homes went under water. The bigger lesson is this: The best use of debt is to buy an asset that retains or increases in value. Else, the asset goes away while you still have the debt to contend with.

If you can think of all debt-financed purchases this way, you'll come out ahead. At least make sure the debt is paid off at the same rate the asset declines, if you do use debt to buy a perishable asset.

In a downturn, using debt at all is riskier, for you don't know what's going to happen to your income. But the fact that asset values are more precarious in bad times makes debt a riskier proposition. At the same time, the value of credit increases during a downturn, for you never know when you may have to use it to save your financial "bacon."

3. Debt is the canary in the coal mine.

This notion was raised in Chapter 8 and bears repeating here: The outcome of doing a lousy job with your short-term finances is, and always is, debt. You have to borrow to make ends meet. So if I see debt—particularly credit card debt where balances aren't paid off monthly—I immediately suspect sloppy finances.

That said, there are some perfectly innocent reasons to have such debt, like an unexpected medical emergency or a job loss, but a car repair doesn't cut it—you should have budgeted a rainy-day fund to take care of it. Okay, maybe sloppy is a bit harsh; how about "room for improvement" instead?

So, the goal of this chapter is to help you make sure that canary keeps singing. You don't want your finances to spiral out of control, especially in a downturn. And as suggested earlier, maintaining good credit is even more important during a downturn. Finally, some credit crises are inevitable, so a strong recovery is important.

The tips in this chapter cover proper use of debt and credit, better ways to manage your credit, and how to recover from a crisis.

Tip #80: Distinguish Between Good Debt and Bad Debt

You thought all debt was bad. Now why make it more complicated by talking about good and bad debt; isn't life complicated enough without having to slice and dice everything into good and bad?

Turns out that debt can be good if used for the right things in the grand financial scheme. If you borrow to buy something (an asset) that grows in value long term, and the long-term growth in value is fairly certain, borrowing can be a sound strategy. Until recently, real estate met this definition, so a mortgage is generally good debt.

THE UP SIDE OF REAL-ESTATE DEBT

The recent downturn in real estate doesn't mean all real-estate debt is bad, in fact, quite the opposite is true. Real estate is still a long-term value, especially your personal residence. Some of the debt recently taken on to buy it may be bad, but that's because the risk incurred with the debt (with ARMs, options, subprime) exceeded the long-term potential of the asset. So good debt can still be used to buy a bad investment—watch out.

Most debt probably falls into the bad category—where the value of the asset purchased declines faster than the debt is paid off. Most credit-card debt probably winds up here. Car loans can be good or bad, depending on the terms of the loan and how fast the car depreciates.

Why Is It Important?

If you have debt left over when the asset is gone, you have a financial burden with no benefit. Worse, you're probably going to replace it with something else—another pair of shoes, another dinner, another vacation—and incur still more debt. It's not hard to see how the debt snowball gets going.

What to Do

Think both sides of the equation. How long will the debt last? How long will the asset last? If the debt is bound to last longer than the asset, think twice about doing it.

Bargains can be okay. Using credit to capture a steep discount—like a 40 percent off sale—can work out; the debt can be good debt because it saved you money. But make sure you really needed whatever it was in the first place.

Pay off bad debt first. Attack bad debt first if you're trying to get back on your feet. Typically, it's the most expensive debt, too, since lenders are less willing to lend cheap when there's no quality asset involved. Generally, you should pay off credit cards first if you can, and pay off the entire balance each month if possible.

Tip #81: Evaluate Your Credit Score

You've probably heard plenty about credit scores by now. It's a secret and squirrelly mathematical judgment of your creditworthiness; that is, your ability and willingness to pay off debts. Effectively it's a financial report card, and it's calculated by all three major credit bureaus (Experian, Equifax, and TransUnion), and most scores are based on mathematical models provided by a company called the Fair Isaac Corporation, known in the trade as FICO.

Why Is It Important?

Your score is used by potential creditors, lenders, as a big-time criteria for deciding whether to lend you money and at what interest rate and terms. If you have a bad score, you'll suffer any time you apply for or need credit. That's particularly true in a weak economy when credit is tightening. What's a bit more surprising is how your credit score has become a general referendum on your character, used well beyond the determination and award of credit. A bad score can hurt you well beyond the banking and credit world in a downturn.

What to Do

Property and casualty insurance. Insurance companies, especially auto insurers, use credit scores to determine your overall financial responsibility; really, your overall responsibility, period. Poor scores can cause insurers to think less of your character and put you into higher rating groups. While they're required by law to tell you, it's perfectly legal to do it.

Employers. It isn't clear that employers actually use your credit score, but they do use your credit report. Up to 70 percent of them do it now according to some reports. Why? Because it's more dependable—and less subject to libel suits—than employer references. If you think you might need a new job, work on your credit score, not just your resume.

Utility companies. Signing up for a new utility service? If your score isn't very good, you're likely to pay higher deposits.

Cell phone and other plan providers. Sort of the same—the best prices and rates go to the strongest customers.

Tip #82: Keep Your Credit Report Up to Snuff

The credit report is the raw data from which your credit score is calculated. It lists your credit history, generally for the last ten years, and includes all credit card and installment-loan activity.

Activity includes loan amounts, credit amounts (the amount you're permitted to borrow), payment history, history of application for credit, and any comments made by previous lenders or creditors. It will include bankruptcies, foreclosures, and related court judgments. It may include employment information, but nothing about your income or wealth. In short, it includes all your transactions—and all your intentions—having to do with credit.

It is a record about you, but you have no direct influence on that record. Each of the three credit-reporting agencies—Experian, Equifax, and TransUnion—keeps a record as sort of a free-form electronic ledger of your credit events. Any creditor can put anything there, and by law, you have no legal control. However, you can and should manage your credit report carefully, for mistakes are common, and can be dealt with using the right approach.

Why Is It Important?

According to various studies, as many as 87 percent of credit reports have an error of some sort. According to the Consumer Federation of America, 31 percent have an error that could take fifty points away from a credit score. That's not a good thing, especially in a downturn when you might really need your credit.

What to Do

Examine your credit report at least annually. By Federal law, you're granted free access to your credit report at least once a year. That doesn't mean you get a free credit *score*—that might cost $8 to $13 extra, but may be worth it. Watch where you go to get the free report, often there are strings attached. The right place to do it is AnnualCreditReport.com—a free service sponsored by the three reporting agencies. Others may ask for personal information or try to sell you something. If you have a friend in the banking or auto finance business, they can check your reports, too, but make sure they do it in a way that doesn't appear as an application for credit, which can hurt your score.

Deal with credit agencies in writing. If you find an error, don't blow your top and pick up the phone to call the agency. Instead, get the facts and write the credit agency or agencies with the bad information. Credit agencies are required by law (Fair Credit Reporting Act) to investigate and make a correction if the facts dictate it. Creditors aren't required to, but they may (and should) help you out. In fact, it's easier if the creditor sees the light and initiates the change so you don't have to make the case. You can sometimes do this with a phone call to the creditor, but experts advise keeping detailed records of who you talked to and what was said.

Be precise and persistent. Keep precise records and don't give up. If there's a mistake, it should be fixed sooner than later, and you'll come out ahead as a result.

Tip #83: Assign Specific Tasks to Your Credit Cards

You're in the mall on a Saturday afternoon. You find a nice pair of jeans that you want, now. You head to the cashier and grab a card. Which card? You just used the Chase VISA yesterday. Bought a tank of gas yesterday—wasn't it the Citibank MasterCard you used? You haven't used the AMEX in a while, so let's use that one.

So what's wrong with this picture? You're using a jumble of cards—and most people have more than three—anytime for anything. Downturn or not, one of the obvious things you can do to manage your credit and debt effectively is to assign a purpose to each card and stick with it, as you'll see below.

Why Is It Important?

When you're in credit-card free-for-all mode, it's almost impossible to keep track of expenses against a budget, save by going online every night to check the balance on each card. So all cards tend to drift out of control.

What to Do

Choose a household card. I suggest every household should have one common card (with multiple users, if necessary) tied to household expenses. This can and probably should include family allowances (Tip #74). This card is used religiously for home maintenance and improvement, family outings, gas and car expenses, vacations, and so forth.

Designate a personal card(s). After household and family allowances are cared for, next is the personal credit card tied to the personal allowance. Each participating family member gets one. If your PAL is $300 a month, then use the card for PAL purchases and track the balance through the month accordingly. You can use any brand of card you want, of course; no-fee cards are best since you'll have more than one.

Select an emergency card. Emergencies happen, appliances break, you name it. I like to keep one extra card around for the unbudgeted expenses. That helps keep the other cards in check with their respective budget—no unexpected bulges. This card should have a low interest rate, since you might be forced, depending on the size of the bulge, to carry a balance. The goal should be no balance and no charges each month.

Tip #84: In Trouble? Decide Whom to Tell

Most of us learn from an early age not to go to a parent or authority figure with bad news. Drop a glass of milk—clean it up and hope Mom and Dad never find out. That same feeling applies to debt, and it's reinforced by the credit reporting and scoring process being seemingly hell-bent on finding and reporting anything bad about you. In a downturn, most creditors are in a bad way, too. So it might seem smart, if you're having problems or think you might have problems, to simply not say anything. So what if you lose your job? Should you tell your creditors? Or should you hide and hope you can keep things going until the crisis blows over?

Turns out, you're probably better off to inform creditors of problems, especially if there's time to do something about them. Call an agent to review your options.

Why Is It Important?

In a credit crisis, most creditors are more focused on getting their money back than dinging you. So they're more likely to work out payment plans, or at least notate your file so you might get a little leniency later on. They can't really ding you, anyway, until you actually miss a payment.

What to Do

Arrange workouts. Some creditors may help you by restructuring your payments or interest rate; for instance, allowing lower minimum payments or none at all, with unpaid amounts added to the balance. Most creditors have special-assistance desks set up to work things out, although if things are really bad, you'll have to be patient and persistent. The earlier you notify creditors, the better.

Look into protection plans. Some credit cards offer protection plans that suspend payments and interest accrual in the event of a job loss and various other benefits. Discover's Payment Protection plan and Citibank/Sears MasterCard's Account Care Plus are examples. They cost a little less than 1 percent of your balance each month, which could be a good value if you feel things might get shaky.

Balance transfers. Especially if you're a good long-term customer, your creditor may allow a balance transfer for other debts into an arrangement with an attractive interest rate. Such a transfer, of course, reduces interest costs, and it puts your debts in fewer places, making them easier to manage.

Be a good customer. If you've been loyal to a creditor, doing business with them for a long time, you're likely to get more flexibility and help. Build a relationship with your creditors, keep everything current, contact them early in advance of trouble, look for the win-win, and be nice.

Tip #85: Five Best Ways to Get Out of Debt

The annals of financial journalism are full of get out-of-debt-stories; you've probably read a dozen or more by now. Most of them make sense, but some are hard to implement or involve producing more income. I'll share a few that, from my experience and that of others, seem to work.

Why Is It Important?

It's no secret that getting out of debt can improve your life and help insulate you from a downturn. But it's hard to break old habits or make temporary adjustments to our standards of living to make these debt-breaking tactics stick. Nobody wants to give anything up, and it's hard to change habits, especially the ones that got us into debt in the first place. So, I'll offer a few short bits of practical advice I think can really help.

What to Do

Cut up the cards. If you can, put your credit cards away altogether. If you can't pay for something, you won't spend! You may find you don't even miss them, and your wallet will be thinner, too. Short of putting them all away, reduce the cards and assign specific tasks to the few still left, as in Tip #83.

Stop spending. Just learn not to spend money, learn to do without, learn to stop bowing to pressure. I drive a seventeen-year-old Ford Explorer; it's a great car, and not replacing it has saved me countless thousands. I do go out with my friends, but if I were in a reduce-debt mode, I'd simply say, "No thanks—I'm trying to cut back." It's cool—if you hang out with the right kind of friends, anyway—especially during a downturn. And when you go somewhere, count every dollar NOT spent. Some of my best vacation days—or trips to the mall—are the ones where I don't spend anything!

Pay off smallest balances first. Want to attack a multiheaded Hydra beast? Chop off as many heads as possible as soon as possible. If you get rid of the little problems, you can focus more on the bigger ones. So if you have ten credit cards: two with very large balances, three with medium ones, and five with very small balances, get rid of the latter five first. Then cut those cards up or put them in a remote dresser drawer.

Then, pay off highest rates. Most financial types will advise paying off the highest rates first. In theory, it makes sense, but it's often easier to pay the small balances first. Do that, then go after the highest interest rates. If the balance is high enough, you might look at a lower rate on a balance transfer, but if you can pay it off in a few months just focus on doing that rather than spending the energy moving it around. Then cut up those cards, too. Extinguish debt, don't just move it around or create fertile ground for regrowth.

Reward yourself and your family. As offered in the last chapter on budgeting, human behavior responds better to a reward system. As your debt dries up, make sure people in your family who sacrifice and contribute to the effort are rewarded. Small tokens of appreciation like gift cards are nice, or a family outing or even a vacation, if finances permit.

Tip #86: Five Best Ways to Improve Your Credit Score

Like the recipe for Coke, the exact formula for determining your credit score is a well-guarded secret. But the Fair Isaac Corporation, the folks who pioneered the credit-scoring concept, offer some clues about what factors and behaviors have the most influence on your score. Not surprisingly, they all have to do with how well you manage your debt and credit. In order:

✔ *Payment history, 35 percent.* Whether you pay on time, have had judgments, foreclosures, bankruptcy.
✔ *Outstanding debt, 30 percent.* How much debt you have, particularly relative to the amount of credit you've been granted.
✔ *Length of credit history, 15 percent.* Do you have a proven track record with your creditors and credit in general?
✔ *Number and type of loans, 10 percent.* Do you have a good mix of credit options—mortgage, car loan, other installment loans, credit cards? Or do you put all eggs in one basket? Diverse is considered better.
✔ *New credit activity, 10 percent.* Have you applied for credit recently? Often? That can be a bad sign.

Why Is It Important?

Your credit score has become your financial report card, and goes beyond to reflect your overall character in the eyes of many. Keeping your score high keeps more credit available at better rates and gives you more flexibility. It helps to know what behaviors hurt or help your score. The bottom line is, stay current, stay stable, and stay loyal.

What to Do

Check accuracy. You pay your bills on time and generally manage credit well. But on checking your score, you're only pulling a below-average 650. So what gives? The raw data used to calculate your score may be off, so the first step is to check the accuracy of your credit report.

Get and stay current for a year. This is hard, especially if you're in crisis mode, but do anything possible to get your payments current for at least a year. Make schedules, keep notebooks, have other family members help, sign up for online bill pay (to reduce postal lag time)—whatever you need to do to get the minimum payments in on time.

Reduce debt-to-credit ratio. The chapter intro talks about the difference between debt and credit and how unused credit is good and debt is bad. The credit score looks carefully at how much debt you've used versus how much you have available, and assumes if you're using most of what's available—even from one source— that's bad. It's best to keep balances below 40 percent of your credit limit for any revolving debt like credit cards. And never go over a limit.

Stay loyal. Creditors favor a long history and customer relationship, and so do the scoring agencies. A long relationship means stability and experience. It's counterintuitive, but advisers suggest keeping old, largely unused accounts open. First, they raise your available credit; second, the scoring gods don't like change and will ding you even if you close accounts (not to mention open new ones). So don't respond to credit card offers, and keep those accounts open (even better, use them once in a while and pay them off; that improves history).

Don't apply for credit unless you really need it. Again, the scoring process favors stability, and regards an application for credit as a possible signal of trouble, especially if there are numerous applications in recent history. Shop rates carefully before applying for anything, and don't respond to offers unless it absolutely makes sense in the big picture.

Tip #87: Between a Rock and a Hard Place—DMPs and Debt Settlement

Things are really tough: you've lost your job and are just barely hanging on. Debts are piling up, as are interest charges and various fees. You feel the acceleration—downhill. What should you do?

Between the rock of massive debt and the hard spot of bankruptcy, there are basically two places you can get help. A Debt Management Plan is the first, put together by an accredited credit counselor who understands your situation and works with you to achieve a plan. With the right amount of discipline and luck, it can work.

If it really doesn't look like you can handle your debt any time in the foreseeable future, you can work out a debt settlement (actually, you have one worked out for you) that serves as sort of a dark win-win, getting you out of a hole while giving your creditors something.

Why Is It Important?

The sooner you can take action, the sooner you can stop the slide and get things moving in the right direction. It's cheaper, creditors and credit agencies will like you better, and you'll feel better about yourself. Again, action is much better than denial-based inaction.

What to Do

First stop: see a credit counselor. If you haven't checked with a credit counselor already, these folks are trained to help people in your situation, and it's normal to approach them in times of crisis. It can't hurt—a talk with a credit counselor doesn't hit your credit record. A good counselor from an accredited nonprofit agency will help you figure out what you can do. They'll help you work out a debt-management plan with specific actions and behaviors designed to help you get back on your feet. Remember, they're on your side; most of your creditors aren't.

Second stop: a debt-settlement company. Special companies exist to help you negotiate a settlement with creditors. You'll want to go here if your debts are too large for your foreseeable income to handle, you're unable to make minimum payments, or have stopped making payments altogether. You'll enter a contract with the settlement company; they'll work with creditors on your behalf. Typical settlements run fifty to eighty cents on the dollar. The best settlement companies are members of the Association of Settlement Companies, or TASC (*www.tascsite.org*).

Get settlement terms. If you go the debt-settlement route, your accounts will be closed and you'll receive settlement terms. You'll usually be allowed to retain one credit card for emergencies or other transactions requiring a card. The company will typically set up a payment schedule over a two- to three-year period—directly to the creditor, not the settlement company (that wouldn't comply with TASC standards). You'll pay a fee, typically either 15 percent of the outstanding balance or 25 percent of the amount reduced, and fees and interest may still accumulate.

The damage is done. You'll take a hit to your credit score, but if you satisfy your agreement, you'll stop the damage and start back on your feet. It's better than bankruptcy, but if you can get by without doing a settlement, you're even better off.

Tip #88: Recover from a Debt Crisis

For otherwise diligent and dignified human beings, there are few things that can leave bigger scars than a major debt crisis. It's usually a combination of external factors and intrinsic behaviors that brings on the crisis; the process is bewildering and the effects on self-esteem are long lasting.

But once a debt crisis is past, it's important to:

✔ Repair the damage
✔ Move on
✔ Learn the lessons
✔ Make sure it never happens again

Don't just go back to business as usual.

Why Is It Important?

Likely, as laid out in Tip #61, you went through some form of grief cycle—denial, anger, bargaining, depression, and acceptance. Maybe there are lingering bits of depression or even anger; it's hard to move on completely. But you need to do so, for your own peace of mind and a healthy financial future.

What to Do

Don't blow it—again. The main lesson of a debt crisis, whether more of the self-inflicted or externally inflicted variety, is to deal effectively with your finances, see trouble coming, and play defense. Like love, those who learn their financial lessons the hard way usually come out better in the end, even with the baggage they may carry around for a period of time.

Say what you're gonna do, do what you say. If you've made peace with the causes of your debt crisis, make a personal (or family) plan to avoid getting into trouble again. Make a budget if you need to, keep your expenses in check, track where you are financially, and confront difficulties head on. But make your commitments and make them clear; don't steer away from them out of convenience or sloppiness. You'll be happier as a result.

Pay your friends back. Somewhere along the way, your friends, family, or even employers helped out: maybe financially, maybe with some advice or encouragement, maybe by providing some free baby-sitting for your kids. Whatever it was, it was valuable, and you should make an effort to repay and reciprocate. You'll feel better, and they'll feel better about helping you.

Remember what's most important. Money isn't everything, and neither are the material things it buys. Remember, there's a lot more to life than money in your pocket or boats in your driveway. Rather than letting your debt crisis tear apart the bonds of family and friendship, use them to bring them together. How? By staying focused on what's *really* important.

Chapter 11

Protect Your Ass(ets)

So far, we've covered how to protect your current lifestyle—how to make ends meet, how to protect your job, how to protect your home. This chapter speaks more to how to protect your future lifestyle—the lifestyle you plan to live years down the road and into retirement.

Unless you plan to work for an ever-growing wage for the rest of your life, the achievement of a desirable lifestyle inevitably involves saving some money. I'll spare you the math, but having enough to live the really decent lifestyle you deserve in your golden years requires a lot of cash—a six- or seven-figure retirement nest egg for most of us.

That's not all; there are goals along the way, like college, a dream house, starting a business, or making an important charitable contribution. Yes, building a nest egg to handle all these things means you have to save, but it also means investing those savings so your money is earning money, not just you. In fact, the older you get, in theory at least, the more your money should earn for you. Your money takes over as the primary earner, while you scale back on what you produce from working.

This is all well and good, in theory at least. Your ship gets larger and larger and gradually comes into port, but we all know it doesn't happen that way in real life, right? First, it's hard to save, hard to put it aside in the first place. PYF is the usual way, but even if you do put it aside, how do you grow it? And when times get bad, how do you protect it? There's nothing worse than the perfect storm of declining income and declining wealth, yet that's what most downturns do to us.

That's what this chapter is about—protecting your wealth, your nest egg, while keeping an eye on future growth. No, it won't be perfect; your boat will take on water, and it might get really ugly for a while. It might get so bad that you stop looking at your brokerage and retirement plan statements for a while—the investing equivalent of ignoring the truths we covered in Parts II and III. It's really about making the best of a bad situation, about staying the course in times of trouble.

This isn't a book on investing, so many topics—and many of your favorite kinds of investments—may be omitted for focus and lack of space.

Tip #89: Shift to Defensive Investing

When things are good, we're all optimists. Our investments—stocks, funds, our home—grew 15 or 20 percent last year, so no reason why they shouldn't this year, right? Wrong. As covered in the Introduction, the economy has cycles. Expansion is inevitably followed by contraction, as excesses in the economy correct. In the long run, the total investment pool can grow no faster than the economy as a whole—2–3 percent in a typical year, 4–5 percent in a good one. Yes, some investments grow faster than that if they do better than the economy as a whole, but that means other investments can—and must—do worse than that, else the whole can't equal the sum of the parts, right?

Theoretical economic discussions aside, you can't assume above-average growth in your assets forever. It just doesn't happen. You must take time out to play defense, to keep some funds in investments that tend to suffer less in a downturn. And you should prepare to shift funds in that direction when you first spot trouble.

So defensive investing involves using defensive investments and taking a defensive approach to managing your assets.

Why Is It Important?

The consequences of not playing defense can be dire. Your assets can jump up and down like a yo-yo. Stressful for sure, and it can be downright painful if you have to fund something, like a college education or a medical expense or a retirement just when things are at their low. Imagine the sixty-four-year-olds in the 2001–2002 downturn fully invested in stocks who suddenly lost 80 percent of their retirement savings, with little chance for recovery.

What to Do

Do the 100 minus your age calculation. There are a million asset-allocation rules out there and I won't go into them—that's a conversation between you and an adviser or for further individual research. But one principle stands above the others: The amount of money you invest in stocks—the growth part of your asset base—as a percentage should be 100 less your age. So if you're twenty-five, 75 percent of your assets should be in stocks; if you're sixty, that percentage should drop to 40, while remainders should probably be in more steady, fixed-income investments.

Keep it in cash. When times get tough (or are about to), the safest place to be is in cash. Cash is king, as they say. Not necessarily 20s and 50s in your mattress, but cash safely tucked in a bank or some other cash instrument like a money-market fund. Aside from inflation, no matter what happens, that cash doesn't lose value. Your money's doubly safe if it's in an FDIC-insured savings account, which are now insured up to $250,000.

Find defensive stocks. There are lots of companies like retailers or RV makers that count on people having lots of disposable income to spend. Disposable income is the first thing to go in a downturn, but people still need food, energy, and medical supplies. As the economy starts to look weak, or overheated in advance of weakening, smart investors shift to the defensive side of the ball.

Go wider, not deeper. Likewise, as the offensive part of the economy weakens, it's usually better to diversify more; that is, have smaller amounts of more different investments. That way, your investments are more likely to track the economy as a whole, not do worse. Likewise, most investors can stay out of trouble by buying large companies like General Electric or Procter & Gamble, with their immense financial resources and experience dealing with downturns. Of course, this doesn't always work, as bank investors can attest to during the 2007—2008 downturn. You must also think about what's causing the downturn.

Get professional help. If you don't use it already, a bad economy can be a good time to turn to the pros, who usually have more experience—and maybe less optimism—than you do.

Tip #90: Stay for the Long Haul

"The market, as measured by the Dow Jones Industrial Average, was down 362 points today, after a 253 point gain yesterday." So says the radio announcer on your way home from work.

Now those are pretty big numbers. Do you want to ride this roller coaster? Probably not, unless you happen to be a professional stock trader. More likely, you do something else, and you want your investments to do something for you over the long haul. What can you expect from different kinds of investments in that haul?

The most common figure you'll hear is this: Stock investments have returned an average of 10.4 percent annually since 1930. Now, how can that be? I just said that long-term growth has to match that of the economy—about 3–4 percent in the average year. Turns out it works, for the 10 percent is about equal thirds dividends and cash payouts, inflation, and real growth. So that, indeed, is what you can expect, for the long haul.

What about shorter periods? I've borrowed a table (see Table 11.1 below) from Ibbotson & Associates, keepers of elaborate records of such things. It takes a lot to fully grasp this table, but comparing returns (mean annual growth, highest quarterly returns) with risk (volatility, number of positive and negative months, and the difference between highest and lowest quarterly returns) quickly paints a picture of which groups of investments are more or less vulnerable to downturns.

Table 11.1: Long Term Performance, Selected Market Indexes, 1988–2007

Index	Mean annual growth	Volatility	Positive months	Negative months	Highest quarterly return	Lowest quarterly return
U.S. large cap stocks	11.8%	15.2%	156	84	21.3%	−17.3%
U.S. small cap stocks	11.4%	19.8%	151	89	29.7%	−24.5%
U.S. REITs	12.3%	14.9%	145	95	22.7%	−14.6%
Foreign stocks–developed	7.8%	17.3%	149	91	20.8%	−21.1%
Foreign stocks–emerging	16.3%	26.9%	156	84	32.6%	−23.6%
U.S. Bonds	7.6%	4.2%	170	69	8.0%	-2.9%

Source: Ibbotson Associates

Why Is It Important?

As a prudent investor, you want to balance the likely reward, or return, against the risk you're taking. You also want to invest for the long haul, as all investments tend to do well, for example, during the most recent twenty years, or longer. As financial planner Jack Everett, CFP®, AIMC says, you want to "rely on time more than timing."

What to Do

Stay in stocks for growth. As you can see, over the past twenty years, U.S. stocks did even better than the long-long-term return of 10.4 percent. But the volatility (15.2 percent) is far higher than bonds (4.2 percent), and when things are bad, they're bad. Incidentally, large-cap stocks are companies with a total market cap (share price times number of shares) greater than $5 billion; small cap are smaller companies with a total value of $1 billion or less.

Bonds—the tortoise racing the hare. Bonds are steadier, but less risk means lower returns.

REITs for real estate. These are real estate investment trusts—special pools investing in real estate. So this line captures the long-term growth and risk of real estate; but keep in mind, this figure is not only residential but also commercial, and the returns are only calculated through the end of 2007.

Foreign stocks have had a mixed track record. You'll hear a lot of advisers and experts talking about investing overseas during a downturn as a matter of safety or protection against a fall in the value of the dollar. I think it's hard to understand foreign investments, and as you can see, the returns aren't too exciting. Better during a downturn is to invest in large U.S. companies that sell a lot overseas—like Hewlett-Packard or General Electric, both with about two-thirds of their business overseas.

What about mutual funds? Not considered here, for they're just a way to buy and sell the assets called out in the table—they aren't an "asset class" themselves.

Tip #91: Bonds, CDs, MMAs—Choose the Best

From this point on, I'll discuss specific defensive investments. This tip covers cash or so-called cash-equivalent or fixed-income investments—relatively low-risk investments designed to preserve your capital and give a modest return. In most cases, they're safer than keeping cash in a mattress, for you don't have to worry about fire!

The biggest thing you do have to worry about is inflation. If a cash-equivalent investment pays 2 percent annual interest, and inflation is 4 percent each year, you lose 2 percent purchasing power each year. So yes, cash is king, and when preservation outweighs the need for growth, cash is the right place to be, but it isn't the only place to be, especially when things improve.

Why Is It Important?

Smart cash investments give the best returns and best defense against inflation, while still protecting against the downturn. And when the economy turns around, it's relatively easy to move money from these instruments into higher-return investments.

What to Do

Regular savings. Just park the cash in your local bank or credit union, or for a little extra return, one of those Internet banks you see advertised all the time. You'll have access to your money at all times, but returns can be exceptionally low, under 1 percent in most cases. Look for good deals from a credit union. Some institutions offer free checking, bill pay, or other benefits if you keep cash around, so it isn't just about interest.

CDs—certificates of deposit. These tie your money up for a little while and get a higher interest rate, maybe 2 or 3 percent higher than a standard savings account. It's 100 percent safe and works, unless you think you might need the money sooner than the term—typically one to five years. In fact, it keeps it out of reach, which can be a good thing.

Money-market funds. So-called MMAs, or money-market accounts, have many names, but are mostly the same thing. For a yield somewhere between a savings and a CD, the funds are liquid, but interest rates rise and fall with the market, and as they aren't FDIC insured, there's a slight risk the value could fall below what you invested if things get really bad for the bank or broker offering the fund. A government money-market fund pays a little less but is safer, and in late 2008, the U.S. Treasury *temporarily* extended protection to all money-market funds. It's worth checking to see if this protection still exists before moving funds to money-market accounts.

Bonds. Bonds are fixed income securities that represent a promise by a company or a government agency—the borrower—to pay you back at a certain time in the future, with interest paid between now and when the bond is paid back. There are many different kinds of bonds, too many to cover here, but bonds can be more or less risky depending on the creditworthiness of the borrower and how long until you're paid back. The first risk is called credit risk; the second is interest-rate risk, for if the payback is over a long time, say twenty or thirty years, a bond can decline in value if interest rates go up. (A bond paying 5 percent is worthless if interest rates are 10 percent, so goes the logic.) In a downturn, safer and shorter (less credit, less interest-rate risk) is better.

Tip #92: The ABCs of FDIC

FDIC stands for Federal Deposit Insurance Corporation, the insurance guaranteeing the safety of most bank deposits. FDIC insurance covers ordinary bank accounts like checking and savings accounts (not money-market accounts) and CDs, up to $100,000 per depositor, per institution—but there are ways to get more of your stash covered.

Why Is It Important?

Not surprisingly, such protection is important during a downturn. The last thing you'd want is to lose your savings to a bank failure, as many did in the Great Depression before this protection existed.

What to Do

Up to $250,000 per depositor, per institution. These amounts were increased in the late 2008 as part of the Emergency Economic Stabilization Act. The intent of FDIC is to cover each unique individual who deposits up to $100,000 in a unique institution—a chartered bank or savings and loan paying into FDIC. Using different names or different branches of the same institution won't help, but if you and a spouse hold an account jointly, that's considered two depositors, so you're covered for $500,000. A third account where you and your spouse are joint tenants also qualifies for coverage. If in doubt about your coverage or your institution, ask.

Up to $250,000 for retirement accounts. If you set up a self-directed IRA in an FDIC-qualified institution, you're covered up to $250,000. By the way, the 2008 Stabilization Act did *not* change the coverage for retirement accounts.

How to protect a million bucks. If you're fortunate enough to have such a sum, divide it up among several institutions. Make sure they're really separate, not one owned by the other. If you have a very large sum, there are services called CDARS that do the dividing for you for a small cut of the interest. CDARS stands for Certificate of Deposit Account Registry Service—check out *www.cdars.com.*

Get to know EDIE. Also handy is the FDIC's Electronic Deposit Insurance Estimator, which lets you check your current or proposed deposit scheme against the rules, telling you clearly what is and what isn't covered. See *www2.fdic.gov/edie.*

And what about SIPC? FDIC doesn't cover investments—stocks, bonds, mutual funds, or even money-market funds. However, the Securities Investor Protection Corporation gives you some protection, up to $500,000 per account, from the failure of a broker, not from the failure of your investments, but if your broker should happen to close its doors for some reason.

Tip #93: Make Safe Investments in Government Securities

Still, unless something really, really goes wrong, fixed-income securities issued by the Federal government are the safest investments around. Why? Because the government can simply print more money to pay them off. State and local governments are safe, too, but not quite as safe—they can go bankrupt, though this doesn't happen very often.

Why Is It Important?

If you're really not sure what to do and want to park some of your hard-earned worth somewhere safe, government securities bought directly or through bond funds can deal with your doubts. It's become quite easy with their direct-sales website, known as Treasury Direct. See *www.savingsbonds.gov* to learn more and to buy.

What to Do

Bonds, bills, notes. You can get almost any kind of Treasury security you want in almost any maturity or denomination. Treasury bills are the most commonly used by short-term defensive investors. They are sold at a discount (meaning you might pay $98 and get $100 back at maturity) for terms up to a year. Notes pay semiannual interest and mature between two and ten years, while bonds are longer term, ten- to thirty-year instruments as purchased from the Treasury. If you purchase them from a third party—a dealer—you can get any maturity you want. Because of the safety factor, rates are fairly low, but can still run 4 or 5 percent on a long bond as of this writing. Note that by buying longer maturities, you still have interest-rate risk, but you've gotten rid of the credit risk by buying from the U.S. government.

Savings bonds. Savings bonds are set up in $25 dollar incre-ments designed for gifts or small savers, and pay lower rates.

TIPS. These special Treasury Inflation Protection Securities not only pay a safe return, but also change in value according to inflation. So in times of higher inflation, they keep your buying power constant, but pay microscopic interest rates in exchange for this protection. If you want safety and inflation protection at a price (low current returns), check out TIPS.

Municipal bonds. These bonds, issued mostly by state and local governments or public agencies, pay higher than Treasury securi-ties because of higher risk, and the interest is deductible for Fed-eral taxes (Treasury securities generally aren't deductible). So the interest in "munis" primarily comes from higher-income earners. It's kind of a dark and murky world; you'll need help to play this one, and many do it through funds.

Tip #94: Learn How to Buy and Sell Stocks in a Downturn

You hardly know how to buy or sell stocks when times are good, let alone bad. Yeah, it's tricky, indeed.

There are three standout concepts to remember about stock market behavior during downturns. First, the stock market is a leading indicator. Professionals buy and sell stocks anticipating the future, so you might see cracks form when things still seem good. And you might see a market roar ahead when it seems like things are at their worst.

Second, markets are emotional and tend to overreact. Nobody willing to step in and buy? Everyone hears that, so it makes mat-ters worse, and we get one of those 300-point selloffs. While things can seem really awful, usually they're treated as worse in the mar-ket than they really are. Look at what happened in the aftermath of the September 11, 2001, terrorist attacks.

Third, and related to the previous two, there are always values in the market—good companies selling for less than they're worth.

Why Is It Important?

I can't cover it all in one tip, but the primary lessons here are:

1. Be rational, not emotional
2. Be patient

The last thing you want to do is sell your stocks at their ten-year low—but it happens all the time. People tend to throw their towels in all at once; the herd mentality produces nasty results. Don't forget, every bear market has recovered, sooner or later.

What to Do

Mutual funds—why and why not. Mutual funds buy securities on your behalf; you buy shares of the fund and participate in gains and income. Advantages include professional management (trained fund managers and stock researchers to do the driving for you) and simplicity. Both can be helpful during a downturn. Disadvantages include high fees—up to 3 percent of your investment each year—and a Wall Street-driven herd mentality among managers that may be just what you were trying to avoid. If you're not sure whether to invest directly or through funds, talk to an adviser, preferably a fee-based or fee-only adviser not paid by selling you funds!

Buy value. When a stock seems incredibly cheap, consider a buy. What's cheap is hard to determine, but if it makes money and seems to do well in the marketplace and everyone loves its products, that's the first clue. Think of the big picture. If Yahoo!'s market cap is $46 billion and Starbucks is $10 billion, and you had $46 billion, would you buy Yahoo! or buy Starbucks and keep the $36 billion in your pocket? Such choices tell you where the value really is. (For much more on the subject of value investing, see my book on the subject, *Value Investing for Dummies*, 2 ed., Wiley, 2008.)

And what about selling? My primary sell rule is this, especially in a downturn: Sell when there's something better to buy. In an up market, other rules may come into play, like selling when you hit a certain price or profit target. Here, you're watching a stock drop and you know why it's dropping, but you still need to ask if there is something else better out there—considering the possibilities for this company, and considering the low returns of CDs, MMAs, etc. Maybe the CD or MMA is the better thing to buy if you really think it will go down further, but don't sell just to sell— make sure you really believe the alternative prospects are better.

Tip #95: Protect Your Portfolio

Multiple-choice question—choose the best answer(s). You've invested in stocks or stock mutual funds. The downturn comes. What do you do?

1. Stop reading the paper, financial portals, brokerage statements
2. Sell everything
3. Sell only the winners
4. Find ways to protect your portfolio
5. Reduce exposure by selling selectively
6. Do nothing
7. Do nothing yourself, let a pro manage it

Not an easy choice, right? I'll rule out the first three right off the bat—ignoring your assets or making such a knee-jerk decision as selling everything usually doesn't work. The sixth choice, do nothing, can be okay if you have a long-term horizon and the downturn is short. The seventh choice may be okay, too, if you're in deer-in-the-headlights mode and don't know where to turn. I'll venture that number 4, protecting your portfolio, and number 5, reduce exposure by selling selectively, are the two best choices— and those are the centerpieces of this tip.

Why Is It Important?

Hard as it might be to watch your falling fortunes, you should still keep your finger on the pulse—maybe not daily, but at least once in a while. Otherwise, bad things can happen you might have been able to avoid. Selling only the winners leaves you with losers—and a tax bill. Selling everything destroys long-term gains and takes you out of the game when the downturn is over. So a well-thought-out strategy, using some of the tools the market offers, probably works best.

The following concepts obviously take more room to discuss than I have here, but make good topics for further reading or conversation with an industry pro.

What to Do

Stop-loss alerts and orders. A stop-loss order sets a floor price for a stock; when the stock trades at that price, a sell order is entered. So you can set a floor, say, 10 percent below the current price, go to work, and leave it alone. Most e-broker platforms allow you to set an alert without entering an order—you'll get an e-mail or some other electronic alert when it happens. The idea is to protect against further losses, although with orders, dealers and traders can see them and may look at your stock as "on sale" for that cheap price—and you'll catch the low of the day. Still, stop-losses are good protection against major blowups and can get you out earlier than the crowd if things get really bad.

Switch to funds or ETFs. Individual stocks are inherently more risky than more diversified baskets of stocks. If you're nervous and just don't know what will happen, switching to a fund, or today's more modern Exchange Traded Fund(s), can help. ETFs trade for almost any broad or narrow stock index you want; you can enter or exit an index cheaply and easily.

Options. Here's the one-minute version: Options are the right to buy or sell a stock at a predetermined "strike" price on or before a set date. A *put* option gives you the right to sell; a *call* option gives you the right to buy. In a downturn, you can buy put options to give yourself insurance against a bigger meltdown. And especially since volatility—an option price driver—is high during uncertain times, you can sell call options on stocks you own (known as writing covered calls). Doing so allows you to collect the option premium, or sales price, as income during the turbulent period. That's it for now, but options can give you a lot of options for managing your investments during a downturn.

Strategic selling. One tactic I've used over time, not knowing exactly which of my "wonderful" portfolio choices to keep in bad times, is simply to prune the tree all around. That is, sell a fraction—maybe 20 percent, maybe half—of everything you own. That reduces exposure, but still keeps you at the table for a recovery. Incidentally, this is a good tactic in good times, too, when you have a lot of winners and want to take profits, but don't know which ones to part with.

Tip #96: Right and Wrong Retirement-Plan Choices

People have a tendency to neglect retirement savings during bad times—and that's generally okay, since no downturn in history has lasted for the long term. However, there are a few things to understand, and possibly, to do, to batten down the hatches.

Why Is It Important?

To develop and protect a long-term lifestyle and standard of living, nothing's more important than your retirement savings, especially as entitlements like Social Security become more stressed and health-care costs become more expensive. While they should be left to grow for the long term, retirement assets should be grown and guarded with your life—even during, maybe especially during, downturns.

What to Do

ERISA protection and qualified retirement plans. "My company might file for bankruptcy. What should I do with my 401(k)? Can they take it? Will it disappear?" Fortunately, the answer is no. The Employee Retirement Income Security Act of 1974 protects your retirement assets in the event of a company's demise. But it must be a qualified retirement plan, one set forth and administered according to Federal law. If you have any doubts, you should contact a company rep to make sure your plan is qualified—especially if you work for a small business. Be aware, however, that these protections do not cover retiree health benefits.

Put fewer eggs in one basket. You love your company. You love working there, and think it has a chance to prosper beyond belief. So you put most—or all—of your 401(k) or other plan assets in company stock. That idea has worked, but it's dangerous. Imagine if you're wrong—your job goes away and so does your retirement. Most pros suggest putting no more than 20 percent of your retirement in company stock.

Go conservative, but not too conservative. When the downturn flags are flying, it might be time to take a little money off the aggressive-growth table and park it in conservative plan options or even fixed-income investments, like bonds. But don't do too much of this, or keep it there for long. Your retirement assets depend on long-term growth; fixed-income investments barely keeping up with inflation (especially after fund and plan fees) won't do it long term.

Keep the powder dry. Only do premature retirement-plan withdrawals as a last, last resort. You'll lose the benefits of steady savings and investment growth. The assets are hard to replace, and if it's a loan, like a 401(k) loan, it can become due and payable at the worst possible time—when you lose your job. Tap all other resources first.

If you're already retired, scale back withdrawals. If you're already depending on retirement assets and are withdrawing funds, cut back your annual withdrawals just a bit, or at least not increase them to cover inflation. Research shows an annual withdrawal rate somewhere around 4 percent of total assets will preserve income through retirement almost 90 percent of the time. But that assumes growing assets; if they aren't growing, the confidence drops, and can drop a lot. Major changes to retirement-investment value or performance suggest a trip to a qualified financial adviser to figure out what's best for you.

Chapter 12

Downsize with Dignity

Without much doubt, at least for the money spent, Americans enjoy the highest standard of living the world has to offer. We enjoy more living space inside and outside of our homes. We enjoy more transportation freedom at less cost. We enjoy more and better food at less cost. We enjoy more merchandise choices at a lower cost. We enjoy more and cheaper travel opportunities. And it's true regardless of the economic situation, at least so far. Even when the economy sucks, Americans enjoy a better standard of living than almost anyone else. That's important to keep in mind as we adjust to any economic downturn.

That said, the opulence of the 1990s appears to be over. We may be in for a period of *modest* and gradual contraction of our standard of living.

Why do I say that? The signs are everywhere, although as of this writing it's unclear how permanent some of them are. World population is increasing, but more than that, some of the largest population centers—namely China and India—are breaking out. Really, they're breaking forward, from years of very limited living standards. Partially driven by the "flat" world and increased availability of goods, and partially driven by new expectations arising from seeing how the rest of the world lives, these populations and others are craving more of the comforts we in America have long taken for granted.

The higher standard of living for greater numbers of people means there's less to go around for many of us who once had more. The most obvious signs are recent price increases for mainstream commodities like oil, corn, meat, and other food staples. There's only so much to go around, and more demand with steady or only gradually increasing supplies means higher prices.

Higher prices bring economic turmoil, for disposable income people once had to spend on big houses and cars now gets spent at the gas pump and grocery store. So the economy suffers. There's another force at work, too, which may further dampen our standard of living; namely, the problems and shortages in the public sector. Public debt is at an all-time high, and deficits and debts continue to mount. Entitlements like Social Security and Medicare will take a bigger slice of our economic pie, not to mention health-care costs in general.

It all sounds pretty grim, but we Americans are a resilient bunch and there's always been some good news, like advances in technology and productivity, to offset some of these problems. People thought the energy shortages and political turmoil of the 1970s spelled doom, but in the end, they didn't.

We'll all come out okay, but the definition of success might change. We might be in for a period where those who can adapt to new realities best will prosper the most. One where those that live smart rather than living big will come out ahead. In that vein, I suggest one response to a downturn—and perhaps a smart move even into better times—is to "downsize with dignity."

What does that phrase mean, exactly? It means cutting back—a little. It means doing it in smart ways so that you preserve your sense of worth—heck, you might even find a more satisfying lifestyle. Chuck the McMansion, move into the city from the exurbs to a smaller place; now there's more to do and less time spent in frustrating traffic and commutes. It's about cutting waste and unnecessary expenses out of your life, about simplifying, about trying alternatives. We can look at our European counterparts, who for years have lived nice lives in multiunit flats, driving small cars, eating local foods, using public transportation, and generally avoiding the excesses of consumerism. Or we can just sit back and figure out what it means, and what it takes, to live better with less.

Tip #97: Rightsize Your House

In Tip #54, I shared some material recently published by author David Bach on the average size of new homes—which has grown from 1,200 square feet in 1973 to some 2,500 square feet today—and that 23 percent of new homes exceed 3,000 square feet.

That's just huge—on a world stage, on *any* stage. Do we really need 500 square foot bedroom or 200 square foot bathroom suites? Or a 900 square foot "formal living room" with 16 foot ceilings just to show off our finest furniture and china collection? Guest rooms? Play areas? Offices? (Okay, I might make an exception for that one.) It's space many of us have grown accustomed to, but we don't really need it.

Here's the deal—it's not about show anymore—if it ever was. Interestingly, about 100 years ago America went through a similar crisis, where the excesses of the Gilded Age were walked out the door alongside the robber barons that perpetrated them—the

Rockefellers, Morgans, Vanderbilts. Gone were the gaudy, over-sized mansions of the Victorian Age, to be replaced for the next thirty years by the understated elegance and the back-to-basics notion of the Arts & Crafts movement and the Craftsman home style. Are those homes big? No, they're efficient and smart—and many are well located in their urban areas. That's why Craftsman bungalows and their style have enjoyed a resurgence. It's not that you must go out and find a Craftsman bungalow of your own. The message is simply—as it was 100 years ago—big and fancy isn't always best.

Why Is It Important?

Living smart, efficiently, and below your means is always bet-ter than living ahead of yourself, especially in a downturn. If you start learning how to live smaller and more efficiently now, you'll save money in the short term and be ready when the next oppor-tunity to move presents itself.

What to Do

End your McMansion era. Most of us don't need supersized houses or cars. Sure, when energy's cheap, when home prices are rising, when utility costs are steady or declining as a percentage of income, fine; but when things go the other way, look out.

Location, now more than ever. Four-dollar gasoline and long commutes don't mix. Location used to be something discussed in terms of living in the "right" cities or the "right" areas of a city socioeconomically. Now, location takes on a new dimension, one driven by practical matters of shorter commutes and smaller but high-quality homes using less gas and electricity.

Go not-so-big. Again, big and fancy can be far from best. It's time to think about what you really need to accommodate your lifestyle, maybe a slightly downsized lifestyle absent of certain toys taken for granted as needs. A 40" flat-screen TV might do as well as a 58" one—if the room were smaller. Try to imagine—even draw pictures—of the house or floor plan that would really suit your needs, with the quality you've always had, just not the quantity. You don't have to move there today, especially if you own, but it makes sense to start thinking in that direction.

Find alternative housing styles. Builders are sensitive to current trends—smart ones, anyway. There are alternatives to oversized houses, more and more of them as time goes on. One is manufactured housing (not mobile homes, but modular homes). These are high-quality factory-built homes assembled on site—check out Modular Today (*www.modulartoday.com*) and other sites. Another is the eco-friendly and size-friendly green developments or enclaves emerging in several areas.

Tip #98: Make the Tradeoffs: Retirement Versus Everything Else

Tip #96 in the last chapter reiterated the importance of retirement planning and saving. As corporate pensions go by the wayside and Social Security deals with its strains, someday we will all be more responsible for our standard of living than most folks who are retiring today or have retired recently. Managing your finances during a downturn often means trading off current lifestyle support for support for that unknown—and likely longer—future called retirement.

Why Is It Important?

Simply, retirement should come first. If you don't have what you need at retirement, there's no way to get it, and you can't borrow your retirement. That puts extra pressure on you in a downturn to get by with what you have and leave retirement assets alone—even if it means having your lifestyle take it on the chin for a while.

What to Do

Plan and fund your retirement, first. Keep those retirement savings contributions going, if possible. If you must shut them off,
make clear deals with yourself and your family to replenish. You
can borrow for a lot of things—even a college education—but you
can't borrow for retirement.

Map out your retirement lifestyle. Especially if it's not too far in
the future, try to visualize how you'll really live. That ocean-view
home near the seventeenth green at Pebble Beach would be nice,
but what do you really need, especially considering you'll have
more freedom to travel? Come up with downsized alternatives:
living with other family members if it makes sense, living in a
motor home, or even on a college campus (it's been done). Realistic expectations in retirement lead to realistic expectations before
retirement, and if you can reduce your savings burden, that will
help, too.

Consider all alternatives, even outside the U.S. Many folks are
doing quite well living in Mexico, Costa Rica, or Panama. Don't
think that retirement necessarily has to be in the U.S. Put "retire
in Costa Rica" into your favorite search engine; you'll quickly see
what I mean. The world is flat now—take advantage.

Tip #99: Stay Healthy—It Pays More Than You Think

For some of us, the notion of staying healthy connects with the
idea of downsizing, literally. But in a larger sense, eating right and
especially getting some exercise leads to good health outcomes,
and good financial outcomes, too.

Why Is It Important?

America spends $2 trillion on health care annually; almost
$6,700 per man, woman, and child in the country, more than 15
percent of GDP and a figure expected to approach 20 percent by
2016. That's expensive, and it's huge. But on an individual basis,

I've seen (and experienced) a major difference in financial and career outcomes for individuals who work to maintain their health compared to those who don't.

During a downturn, exercise can really make a difference. If you're resourceful and creative, it's free, or nearly so. It increases your productivity and sense of self-esteem, and it will likely reduce your health care costs now and in the future. So I maintain that a downsize-with-dignity program includes exercise, literally for the waistline, and more figuratively, for overall health.

What to Do

Stop smoking, of course. Poor health, higher insurance premiums, and $5 or so per pack—it simply makes no sense. The stress of a downturn may induce you to smoke more, so go the other way, and use any job dislocation as a chance to change habits and quit.

Lose weight. Exercise clears the mind and clears the body, and a clear mind and body work more efficiently. That's part of what creates better financial outcomes—you feel better, you feel better about yourself, and you perform better on the job. Feeling better about yourself may make you more content with what you have, and make you buy less.

Tip #100: Get More Out of It: Buy It Right or Don't Buy It at All

America is a throwaway society; we get tired of what we have. We're concerned about how things look or whether they're in style. We get concerned about how dependable or reliable things are. There are still a lot of people who trade in a car after two or three years, no matter what. Downsizing with dignity may not mean keeping a car for seventeen years (as I have), but a few extra years will save you a lot. Whatever it is—cars, clothing, patio furniture—think about whether you really need to replace it, or buy it at all. There are alternatives, and as America comes to grips with financial reality, many of those alternatives are growing or getting easier.

Why Is It Important?

Buy a three-year-old car, and you'll save up to two-thirds of its value in depreciation (if it's a truck or SUV in 2008). Keep a car longer, and you'll save the depreciation on a new one altogether, not to mention cheaper insurance and no sales tax in sales-tax states. Or don't buy a car at all, if you live in a city served by Zip-Car (*www.zipcar.com*) and only need a car once in a while. And it isn't just cars, you can save a ton if you change your ways to buy smart and get more out of what you have.

What to Do

Buy it used. Clothing at consignment stores; eBay or craigslist when you need a late-model used bike or TV; CarMax for cars—the world is increasingly used-friendly. You don't have to watch the classifieds or go to flea markets or garage sales to find used stuff (although these work, too)—you can find the used stuff you want with just a few mouse clicks.

Rent it. Think you need a pressure washer to clean your house? A carpet cleaner? Dozens of chairs or wineglasses for your next party? Maybe so, but that doesn't mean you need to own and pay for and store and clean and replace all this stuff. Once the domain of professional contractors and other pros, rental yards have all kinds of stuff you might need once in a while. You can use what you want without owning it, and you'll be sure to get the exact number of chairs or wineglasses you need—not too few, not too many.

Keep it longer. That seventeen-year-old car (it's a Ford Explorer, actually) has saved me a ton. My parents traded cars every six years—I figure I've saved almost two whole cars plus a bundle on sales tax, insurance, and registration taxes. Okay, I've spent a little more on maintenance, but it really works out. Don't think you need to replace stuff just because it's getting old.

. . . *or Just Plain Do Without.* I've just never felt the need for a jet ski, boat, RV, camper, swimming pool. Sure, it would be nice, but I've been able to make do without, by renting, sharing with friends, swimming in a nearby lake. Remember, keep telling yourself and your family, life is an experience; it's not about what you have.

Tip #101: Start (Anew) with the End in Mind

I'll close by comparing the financial survival of a downturn with a health crisis. You go through it, endure the pain, start the healing process. Part of the healing process includes realizing how lucky you are to have what you have. Part of it is realizing that, maybe, you need to change your habits or keep your health up better to make sure it doesn't happen again.

When you get through your financial crisis, you'll likely emerge with more realistic, right-sized expectations. You'll realize that happiness is about more than money, and that living with less is okay. Heck, these days, it's even hip, something to be proud of. It's a chance to start again with new expectations, new family agreements, new harmony, and new safeguards against getting caught in the same trap again.

Why Is It Important?

Smoke too much, have a heart attack; keep on smoking, guess what happens? Another heart attack. We're bound to repeat the same mistakes unless we step back and heed the call for change. That's true with finances, not just health.

What to Do

Be cool, be cheap. More and more folks are standing around the water cooler these days bragging about the great deal they got on something—a two-for-one dinner, the special hotel rate they got for their in-town "staycation." When times are good, this is admittedly a bit harder; you feel like a loser crowing about good deals when everyone else has piles to spend. During a downturn, this isn't so much the case; everyone with a brain is running scared. But think again about the good times. Let them spend their money; you'll be smart and better prepared than they will for the next economy that sucks.

Be a role model. Especially if you have children, never forget that what you do makes a lasting impression, especially if they see the reasons you're doing it. If you solve your financial crisis—or even better—prevent it—those that follow you as a role model will "get it," too.

Be proud of what you don't have. Sort of like when I go shopping and feel successful because I didn't buy anything, I also feel pride in being able to do without something. By doing without something, I've effectively earned something else, and I've lowered my stress levels at the same time. So it's not hard for me to give up the $800 weekends and $80 walking shoes—I keep a clear-eyed view of what I've saved, and I can proudly say, "I didn't need that anyway." As a result, I'll have a much better time of it the next time the economy sucks.

APPENDIX A:
List of Resources

These are favorites, but not all the resources I use or mention in the book. Top three in each category:

Websites

General personal finance, financial portals

Yahoo! Finance (*http://finance.yahoo.com*), especially personal finance section

CNN Money (*http://money.cnn.com*)

SmartMoney (*www.smartmoney.com*)

Employment/Career

CareerBuilder (*www.careerbuilder.com*)

Monster (*www.monster.com*)

Quintessential Careers (*www.quintcareers.com*)

Career networking

Weddles (*www.weddles.com*)

Linked In (*www.linkedin.com*)

Efinancialjobs (*www.efinancialjobs.com*)

Unemployment

Department of Labor (*www.bls.gov*)
CareerOneStop (*www.servicelocator.com*)

State sites (search on "unemployment + state")

Foreclosure assistance

HopeNow (*www.hopenow.com*)

U.S. Dept of Housing and Urban Development foreclosure page (*www.hud.gov/foreclosure/index.cfm*)

State sites (search on "foreclosure assistance + state")

Real estate

Realtytrac (*www.realtytrac.com*)

Trulia, especially "stats and trends" page (*www.trulia.com/city*)

National Association of Realtors (*www.realtor.com*—see especially "market conditions" page)

Credit counseling

National Foundation for Credit Counseling (*www.nfcc.org*)

U.S. DOJ Approved Counseling Agencies (*www.usdoj.gov/ust/eo/bapcpa/ccde/cc_approved.htm*)

Newspapers/Periodicals

The Wall Street Journal

The New York Times

USA Today

The Economist

BusinessWeek

Forbes

Books

By Peter Sander:

The 250 Personal Finance Questions Everyone Should Ask (Adams Media, 2005).

The Pocket Idiot's Guide to Living on a Budget, 2ed. (Alpha Books, 2007).

The Ultimate Guide to Personal Finance for Entrepreneurs (Entrepreneur Press, 2007).

By others:

Petrovich, David. *Fight Foreclosure!* (Wiley, 2008).

Sullivan, Bob. *Gotcha Capitalism* (Ballantine Books, 2007).

Tyson, Eric. *Personal Finance for Dummies 5th ed.* (Wiley, 2006).

APPENDIX B:

List of Tips

Chapter 12
Downsize With Dignity

Index